What People Are Saying About

"Everybody talks about marketing with content, but W̶ ̶ ̶vides a systematic approach, SONAR, for actually doing ̶ ̶ ̶g̶ ̶her model you get higher search engine rankings and other results instead of just churning out an endless pile of articles that go nowhere and do nothing."

—Bill Bly, copywriter

"*Content Is Cash* is a classic! We implemented Wendy's SONAR system and saw results (traffic, qualified prospects and opt-in subscribers) within hours, not days or months. It's easy to become overwhelmed with Internet marketing 'advice.' There were more than 26,000 books on Amazon.com this morning dealing with the topic. The SONAR system is not run-of-the-mill advice. You won't find a more complete collection of content marketing anywhere on the planet. Highly recommended!"

—Marc Charles, Entrepreneur, Author, Freelance Guru

"Wendy's book, *Content Is Cash*, is a great book for anyone who wants to leverage their content—publishers, marketers, you name it. It's well organized and explains Wendy's system that can help you build your website and drive a boatload of traffic, and do it in a cost-effective manner. As a writer, I gleaned insight on what kind of articles I should be writing—or what I should emphasize in the articles I'm already writing—to grab eyeballs and hopefully turn them into more sales for my company."

—Sean Brodrick, Editor, UncommonWisdomDaily.com

"This book brings the urgent and swirling noise of contemporary marketing strategy and tactics all together. Wendy has written a practical, no nonsense guide to improving sales and marketing results for any size company. It takes contemporary marketing to a whole new level. Her proven SONAR model is easy to grasp and her style is easy to follow. This should be the next book every Chief Marketing Officer should read. And start banking the results."

—Christopher C. Binkert, Chief Marketing Officer
Soundview Communications, Atlanta, GA

"When it comes to marketing online, content is an afterthought for far too many marketers. It's a pity because, as Wendy Montes de Oca points out in her new book, content can be a huge source of income for any business. That's why I love that Wendy has comprehensively explained dozens of ways to leverage content for an online business. The best part is that—like the pro direct marketer she is—Wendy's strategies are all trackable and quantifiable. So you know exactly how valuable your efforts are to your business."

—Jason Holland, Associate Publisher, *Early to Rise*

"Wendy's insights are priceless and have the ability to payoff in a big way. *Content Is Cash* is a must read for anyone tasked with driving more traffic and revenue in an increasingly more competitive online environment. I'm looking forward to implementing many of her tips, tricks and tactics in my own business immediately."

—Julie McManus, President, Julie McManus Marketing Associates, Inc.

"Content is the single most important factor in building a thriving web business and no one drives that point home better than Wendy Montes de Oca. In *Content Is Cash* she takes the mystery out of putting your content to work for you. Anyone trying to build traffic, sales, or leads would be a fool to not have a copy of this go-to reference on their desk."

—Alice Wessendorf, Managing Editor, HealthierTalk.com

"Wendy's book is an impressively thorough account of the marketing options open to Internet businesses today. I have it within reach of my desk and I intend to make good use of it."

—Michael Masterson, Publisher, Agora, Inc., *Early to Rise*

"Absolutely packed with useful, important information, just what you'd expect from Wendy Montes de Oca"

—Dr. Jonny Bowden, PhD, CNS, JonnyBowden.com

"Wendy told me about the SONAR system almost two years ago, and swore me to secrecy. Now she has done far more than just reveal the SONAR system. In *Content Is Cash*, Wendy gives you a complete blueprint for the *right way* to use free content. I especially recommend *Content Is Cash* to anyone who has tried using free content and been frustrated. Follow Wendy's proven method, and you'll have the cure for what frustrated you."

—Conrad Hall, Best-Selling Author, Speaker, Radio Host
Conrad Hall Copywriting, LLC

"Whenever I think about monetizing content, the first person that comes to mind is Wendy Montes de Oca. I've personally used just one of her strategies in this book to generate thousands of leads and establish instant authority in my niche. *Content Is Cash* is a must have in serious online marketer's library."

—Brian T. Edmondson, Internet Marketing Expert,
   TripleYourProfits.com

"Wendy's new book *Content Is Cash* is exactly what is needed in today's turbulent business world. By reading and putting the tactics and strategies into action, you will position yourself for more profits and a stronger a business."

—MaryEllen Tribby, Founder/CEO WorkingMomsOnly.com

"If you want to transform content into some very substantial money for your business, this must-read book will show you exactly how."

—Martin D. Weiss, Ph.D., bestselling author

What People Are Saying About Wendy Montes de Oca

"Wendy has already met and exceeded my expectations. Her marketing expertise is unparalleled. I can't wait to go on from here."

—Bob Bly, renowned copywriter and best-selling author, Bly.com

"Working with Wendy was one of the best business decisions I made this year…Wendy was a reservoir of creativity, thoughts, and ideas with her marketing strategies, web design, and copywriting magic."

—Karen Keller, Ph.D., Karen-Keller.com

"Wendy is the Neiman-Marcus of Internet marketers. She's a veritable 'one-stop shopping' center for virtually every service you could want or need that involves getting your name and brand out to the marketplace, from copywriting to SEO. What's even more important is that she does all of them well."

—Dr. Jonny Bowden, best-selling author and nutritional healing expert, JonnyBowden.com

"When it comes to the best marketing consultants out there, Wendy's at the top of a very short list. She has the skills, resources, and connections to get the job done—whatever it is."

—Len Bailey, copywriter, LEB Marketing

"Wendy is a creative, strategic thinker, and an implementer who gets the job done with success."

—Chris Ruddy, CEO and publisher, Newsmax.com

"I highly recommend Wendy for any marketing, business development, Internet project, or list-building venture. I'm serious. I've worked with hundreds of direct marketing professionals, gurus, and company principals over the last 25 years. Wendy is in the top 2%!"

—Mark Smalley, owner, Mark Smalley Direct

"Wendy is a brilliant direct response and online marketer with innovative ideas for increasing revenue and generating website traffic and prospects. Her tactics were cutting edge and they worked! She catapulted marketing in equity research and helped both institutional and retail sales."

—Matthew Quinn, Citigroup (formerly Salomon Smith Barney)

"Wendy Montes de Oca simply knows Internet marketing better than any person I have ever encountered. What I have learned is that Internet marketing is both a science and an art, but rarely does one person have both skills. Wendy has a formal background in marketing, a keen eye for analysis, and a creative flair second to none."

—Dave Copeland, president and founder, AppleBoost Products, Inc.

For more about Wendy, visit http://www.precisionmarketingmedia.com/testimonials.html.

CONTENT IS CA$H

Leveraging Great Content and the Web for Increased Traffic, Sales, Leads and Buzz

Wendy Montes de Oca, M.B.A.

800 East 96th Street,
Indianapolis, Indiana 46240 USA

Content Is Cash: Leveraging Great Content and the Web for Increased Traffic, Sales, Leads, and Buzz

Copyright © 2012 by Wendy Montes de Oca

All rights reserved. No part of this book shall be reproduced, stored in a retrieval system, or transmitted by any means, electronic, mechanical, photocopying, recording, or otherwise, without written permission from the publisher. No patent liability is assumed with respect to the use of the information contained herein. Although every precaution has been taken in the preparation of this book, the publisher and author assume no responsibility for errors or omissions. Nor is any liability assumed for damages resulting from the use of the information contained herein.

ISBN-13: 978-0-7897-4108-0

ISBN-10: 0-7897-4108-3

Library of Congress Cataloging-in-Publication Data

Montes de Oca, Wendy.

  Content is cash : leveraging great content and the web for increased traffic, sales, leads, and buzz / Wendy Montes de Oca. -- 1st ed.

  p. cm.

Includes index.

ISBN 978-0-7897-4108-0

  1. Internet marketing. 2. Marketing--Computer programs. 3. Strategic planning--Computer programs. I. Title.

  HF5415.1265.M658 2011

  658.8'72--dc23

2011020685

Printed in the United States of America

First Printing: August 2011

Trademarks

All terms mentioned in this book that are known to be trademarks or service marks have been appropriately capitalized. Que Publishing cannot attest to the accuracy of this information. Use of a term in this book should not be regarded as affecting the validity of any trademark or service mark.

The SONAR Content Distribution Model™ is a registered trademark of Wendy Montes de Oca.

Warning and Disclaimer

Every effort has been made to make this book as complete and as accurate as possible, but no warranty or fitness is implied. The information provided is on an "as is" basis. The author and the publisher shall have neither liability nor responsibility to any person or entity with respect to any loss or damages arising from the information contained in this book.

Bulk Sales

Que Publishing offers excellent discounts on this book when ordered in quantity for bulk purchases or special sales. For more information, please contact

U.S. Corporate and Government Sales
1-800-382-3419
corpsales@pearsontechgroup.com

For sales outside of the U.S., please contact

International Sales
international@pearson.com

Editor-in-Chief
Greg Wiegand

Acquisitions Editor
Rick Kughen

Development Editor
Rick Kughen

Managing Editor
Sandra Schroeder

Project Editor
Mandie Frank

Copy Editor
Krista Hansing Editorial Services, Inc.

Indexer
Tim Wright

Proofreader
Water Crest Publishing, Inc.

Technical Editor
Jackie Stone

Publishing Coordinator
Cindy Teeters

Designer
Anne Jones

Compositor
Studio Galou, LLC

CONTENTS AT A GLANCE

TABLE OF CONTENTS

Foreword

All the Internet gurus today would agree that the key to online success is to market with content. But unfortunately, not many people know how to fully and adequately leverage their content for optimum results.

I've seen it happen many times with marketers, business owners, and entrepreneurs. They try to use article marketing, to no avail. They then conclude that marketing with content doesn't work. They couldn't be more wrong.

You see, the problem is the lack of a systematic method for "syndicating" content and taking article marketing to the next level: getting it in front of as many eyeballs as possible and driving traffic to your website.

And that's the missing link and the key to unlocking the power of great content and the Web. Wendy has cracked the Internet code with her low-cost, high-performing SONAR Content Distribution Model™. It's like article marketing on steroids!

Wendy is the best-kept secret on the Internet today, the consultant behind much of my Internet success...and the success of some of the most well-known and respected publishers in the industry. She brought her "New York gusto" to Florida nearly a decade ago and completely changed the way many top publishers market online. Her concepts were so admired that, aside from her daily marketing leadership responsibilities, she often trained marketing staff, held offsite meetings, and spoke at industry events regarding her proven strategies.

When Wendy left her vice president role at one of the country's top publishers, Agora Inc., I was one of the first people to scoop her up for consulting work. I knew she would become a hot commodity as a freelancer, and I was right. Wendy's business quickly grew with new and referral clients...and more than three years later, it's still going strong.

I've known Wendy for many years now. I've seen her lead large and small online publishers to success with her breakthrough marketing concepts and the innate skill of being "strategically creative." She's an out-of-the-box thinker who gets results. Quite simply, her expertise is unparalleled.

Wendy's *SONAR* system is powerful yet simple. Whether you're a Fortune 500 or start-up company, SONAR principles are easy to implement, with virtually no ancillary costs. SONAR was one of the tactics that helped grow a popular online publisher's list to more than 300,000 subscribers. It also helped build a new alternative health publication's list to nearly 30,000 subscribers in only three months.

I've seen firsthand how this unique and systematic method leverages something most websites have (content) to increase awareness and traffic. I was so impressed with Wendy's SONAR approach on my own business, that I interviewed her for a two-day teleseminar. My subscribers absolutely loved it! I received emails from attendees saying the strategy was "excellent…superb…and an invaluable marketing tool that all business owners or entrepreneurs should have."

And that's because the SONAR Content Distribution Model™ really works.

If you could give your business a boost for virtually no cost, wouldn't you want to learn how?

Get ready, because you won't be disappointed!

—Robert W. Bly

Best-Selling Author, Copywriter, Consultant, and Owner of CTC Publishing

Bly.com

About the Author

Wendy Montes de Oca, M.B.A, has a diversified background that includes nearly 20 years of experience in marketing, media, financial services, and law. She has a proven track record with both acquisition and retention efforts, as well as has both editorial and copywriting success. Her specialties include multichannel marketing (print, Web, email, direct mail, radio, and TV), with expertise in Internet marketing. During her career, Wendy has generated more than $150 million in total revenues for various corporations, consulting clients, and her own consulting firm, *Precision Marketing and Media, LLC.*

Wendy has led the marketing efforts for many prominent organizations. For one online publisher, in only three short months, her search engine optimization (SEO) and lead-generation tactics increased website traffic ranking and visits by more than 3,160% and 62%, respectively, as well as traffic monetization that resulted in a return on investment of 221%.

She previously was the editor of a quarterly investment newsletter and has had several investment articles published in *Hometown News.* Her marketing articles have appeared in popular newsletters, websites, and blogs, such as *Target Marketing, Early to Rise, Makepeace Total Package,* and many more.

Wendy is an advisory board member for Bob Bly's TheLandingPageGuru.com, as well as a distinguished speaker/moderator at prominent marketing conferences such as Specialized Information Publishers Association (SIPA).

Her blog, MuscleMarketing.Blogspot.com, was named top Internet marketing blog by industry staple Best of Web.

Wendy has worked as a strategic marketing consultant and was the force behind the marketing efforts for several top publishers, entrepreneurs, and Fortune 500 companies, including Weiss Research & Publishing, Weiss Money Management, Newsmax Media, Chase Manhattan Bank, General Electric (GE), Automatic Data Processing (ADP) Retirement Services, and Salomon Smith Barney/CitiGroup.

Before starting her successful consulting firm, *Precision Marketing and Media, LLC,* Wendy was vice president of marketing and business development for the Internet's most popular wealth and success e-zine, *Early to Rise* (Agora Publishing), where her online marketing tactics and product development efforts helped bring in thousands of new subscribers and earned millions of dollars in revenues.

Wendy's groundbreaking online marketing strategies have been cultivated and taught to clients, colleagues, friends, freelancers, and former employers spanning the copywriting, publishing, financial, and health industries. She has often trained internal staff or led offsite group sessions to share her online marketing knowledge of increasing website traffic, visibility, leads, and sales. And because her web marketing tactics have been so cost-effective, creative, and successful, Wendy became known as "the marketing maven" by many of her industry peers.

Wendy earned a Bachelor of Science degree from St. John's University and a Master of Business Administration degree from Nova South Eastern University.

Throughout her career, she has been recognized with various awards for quality, innovation, teamwork, and new product/new business development.

Wendy lives in South Florida with her husband of more than 10 years and their son. *Precision Marketing and Media, LLC*, is headquartered in the Palm Beach area of Florida, with satellite offices in the New York City/New Jersey tri-state area.

- For more information, visit www.PrecisionMarketingMedia.com.
- To read Wendy's blog posts, visit www.MuscleMarketing.blogspot.com.
- To sign up for Wendy's free newsletter, *Precision Marketing*, visit www.PrecisionMarketingMedia.com/newslettersignup.html.
- Follow Wendy on Twitter at http://twitter.com/PrecisionMktg.
- "Like" Wendy's Precision Marketing Media, LLC, Facebook fan page at www.Facebook.com/#!/pages/Florida/Precision-Marketing-Media-LLC/139310392787888.

Dedication

This book is dedicated to my loving husband, Jose, who complements my life and broadens my horizons through art, culture, travel, insight, and debate. Jose, you keep me on my toes yet keep me grounded. And to my adorable son, Matteo, who truly is a gift from God, you will always be my "little mijo." Thank you both for fulfilling my life with love and happiness. I feel blessed every day.

Acknowledgments

Sincerest thanks to my mother, Lorraine, and my brother, Chris, who always remain close in my heart, although many miles are between us.

Thank you to my dear friends Maggie Willard Cuello and the entire Staten Island Campus "St. John's University Library Crew" ('89–'91), especially Matt Quinn. You've all known me for a long time and have always believed in my abilities.

Thanks to Ana Villamar for helping out around the house so I can get my writing done.

Thank you to my clients for your professional partnership and trust—as well as for allowing me to lead your business to the next level.

Many thanks to my colleagues who, over the years, influenced me in one way or another on my professional journey: Marilyn Strand, Mark H. S. Cohen, Ian Sheridan, Martin Weiss, Ph.D., Christopher Ruddy, MaryEllen Tribby, and Mark Ford.

Thanks to my special friends at Early to Rise, including Jason Holland, Jessica Kurrle, and Sarah Snoots, who helped distribute my marketing articles to their fabulous list of subscribers.

Thank you to the following clients and companies for helping bring this book to life by allowing me to use their real-life marketing examples for illustrative purposes: Dave Copeland (AppleBoost/Nutrition Intelligence Report), Suzanne Dixon (AppleBoost/Nutrition Intelligence Report), Bob Bly (Bly.com), Karen Keller, Ph.D. (Karen-Keller.com), Dr. Jonny Bowden (JonnyBowden.com), Jason Holland (EarlyToRise.com), and Maria Dolgova (TotalHealthBreakthroughs.com).

Thanks to the following editors and publishers for taking time and sharing with me their real thoughts on what makes great content: Michael Masterson (Agora, Inc.), Jason Holland (Agora, Inc./Early to Rise), Brian Kurtz (Boardroom, Inc.), Chris Ruddy (Newsmax Media, Inc.), Steve Kroening (Second Opinion), Alice Wessendorf (Healthier Talk), Sean Brodrick (Uncommon Wisdom Daily; Weiss Research, Inc.), Dr. Jonny Bowden (In Step with Jonny: Straight Talk Nutrition for the 21st Century), and Bob Bly (The Direct Response Letter). Special thanks to Curt Wilcox (Real Magnet) for passing on some important industry information and best practices.

An additional note of thanks to my friend Bob Bly for writing the Foreword to this book. I've enjoyed the many years we've worked together and anticipate many great collaborations in the future!

We Want to Hear from You!

As the reader of this book, *you* are our most important critic and commentator. We value your opinion and want to know what we're doing right, what we could do better, what areas you'd like to see us publish in, and any other words of wisdom you're willing to pass our way.

As an associate publisher for Que Publishing, I welcome your comments. You can email or write me directly to let me know what you did or didn't like about this book—as well as what we can do to make our books better.

Please note that I cannot help you with technical problems related to the topic of this book. We do have a User Services group, however, where I will forward specific technical questions related to the book.

When you write, please be sure to include this book's title and author, as well as your name, email address, and phone number. I will carefully review your comments and share them with the author and editors who worked on the book.

Email: feedback@quepublishing.com

Mail: Greg Wiegand
                  Editor-in-Chief
                  Que Publishing
                  800 East 96th St.
                  Indianapolis, IN 46240 USA

Reader Services

Visit our website and register this book at informit.com/register for convenient access to any updates, downloads, or errata that might be available for this book.

Introduction

I've worked for some of the top newsletter publishers in the U.S., and I realized two things early on:

Content is king...and content is cash.

The free content (e-zines and e-newsletters) these publishers created was more than a tool to bond with subscribers. And it was much more than a product— albeit a newsletter or paid report. Truth be told, its value hadn't really been tapped into or harnessed until it was looked at from a broader angle and through the eyes of a direct response marketer.

As a direct marketer for nearly 20 years specializing in online marketing, I'm always looking for strategic and creative ways to leverage the one thing my employers or consulting clients seem to have a lot of: content.

I'm also looking for ways to do it in the most cost-effective way possible. Although many of my former employers had decent marketing budgets, I always tried to employ as many low- to no-cost tactics as possible, leaving money for pay-per-click or online advertising efforts, and only when totally necessary to build the business.

Now, being a Type A personality and a Myers-Briggs ENTJ (extravert, intuitive, thinking, judging) helps me tackle all tasks from a very logical, pragmatic, methodical, concise, and efficient way. Building a marketing strategy around leveraging editorial content on the Web is no exception. I needed to think of ways to use the content at my fingertips for multiple purposes—simultaneously. My main objectives were these:

- Prospecting (lead generation)
- Increased website visibility
- Increased website traffic
- Sales

I looked at existing strategies and principles I'd used over the years and thought about how I could use the content resources I had access to in these platforms. I left nothing out, including direct response marketing, search engine marketing (SEM), social media marketing (SMM), search engine optimization (SEO), article marketing, online press releases, market research, and guerrilla marketing.

I discovered that the opportunities were endless. Using content as part of our marketing plans could achieve many goals:

- Help with SEO and website visibility
- Create buzz
- Reinforce credibility
- Drive website traffic
- Promote lead generation
- Inspire like-minded readers to take action
- Drive sales

Even better, the efforts being deployed were quantifiable. Being quantifiable—or measurable—is a fundamental principal for any direct response marketer.

So, I developed a systematic approach to finding content in areas many publishers never imagined. I then created a manual process for repurposing the content and disseminating it to targeted locations on the Web in a synchronized manner. That's when the SONAR Content Distribution Model™ was born.

SONAR represents the following online marketing distribution platforms (or channels):

S Syndicate partners, content syndication networks, and user-generated content sites

O Online press releases

N Network (social) communities and social bookmarking sites

A Article directories

R Relevant posts to blogs, forums, and message boards

I originally wrote about SONAR on my blog, MuscleMarketing.Blogspot.com, back in June 2007. Then I shared what I had discovered with the marketing team I was leading at the Internet's most popular wealth and success e-zine, *Early To Rise (ETR)*, and put it to practical use. To expand its reach even further, I republished my SONAR blog post in ETR's newsletter, exposing it to more than 300,000 eager subscribers.

The feedback I received was tremendous. I then spoke about SONAR at well-known industry conferences such as the Specialized Information Publishers Association (SIPA) and even conducted a teleseminar about it with direct marketing and copywriting legend, Bob Bly.

I was so excited about my findings, the results, and the accolades that I wanted to share SONAR with as many people as possible: marketers, editors, bloggers, publishers, entrepreneurs, freelancers, business owners, and more!

Businesses large and small were all salivating about this easy-to-implement strategy that didn't involve much time—and, even better, didn't involve much (if any) money.

I've been on this mission for the past three years or so, trying to spread the word about something that actually works during a decade when everyone seems to claiming to be the next "Internet guru" and wanting to charge you an arm and leg just to give you some theories.

SONAR is not a theory; it's an established strategy. In an economic climate in which companies are closing down left and right, business owners are searching for a real solution to save their businesses—and a way to do it economically.

SONAR is not a theory; it's an established strategy.

That's where I am today, sharing this proven, powerful, and cost-effective web content marketing strategy in the most prominent forum possible: a book.

The best part of SONAR is that you don't have to be a marketing genius to implement it. Anyone from novice to expert can take advantage of SONAR. Any website with content, whether it's contextual, audio, or video, has the ability to ultimately turn traffic into sales.

What's in This Book

Inside this book, you'll discover that it doesn't take a lot of time or money to build your website and drive a boatload of traffic through an easy-to-learn and wildly successful strategy called the SONAR Content Distribution Model™.

SONAR is the synchronized distribution of content in a systematic and targeted way that will help boost your business for little-to-no advertising cost. Each letter in SONAR represents a free online channel in which your content will be disseminated.

This effective, yet efficient, model will show you step-by-step how to leverage your content (whether it's contextual, audio, or video). This model also will help you find content you never even thought of using—in a comprehensive way that will gain you increased website visibility, traffic, and buzz. Even better, you'll learn how to harness the additional website visits and exposure for lead generation and sales.

SONAR is not a theory, but a proven strategy that gets results.

> This effective, yet efficient, model will show you step-by-step how to leverage your content...

Find out what the ideal SONAR website looks like and discover the "blueprint" to building your own SONAR site. You'll learn hot tips on how to implement SONAR for your own business as well as how to master each of SONAR's critical components including article marketing, online PR, social media marketing, search engine marketing, search engine optimization, and guerrilla marketing (covert marketing in relevant blogs, forums, and message boards). You'll also learn how to measure your SONAR efforts, see some real-life performance history, and get the "inside secrets" to other components in your online marketing mix, including online advertising and media buying, affiliate marketing, joint ventures, and ad swaps.

As a special bonus—in addition to learning my SONAR Content Distribution Model™, you'll also get a broader perspective from my friends and respected colleagues. Learn the inside scoop on what makes great content that gets read and passed around as well as other business "must do's" from some of the top publishers and editors in the industry, including Boardroom Inc., Agora

Inc./Michael Masterson, Early to Rise, Newsmax Media, Inc., Soundview Publications, Inc., Bob Bly, and more.

Whether you're a novice or an expert—this book is the ultimate Internet marketing tool and the ONE and ONLY book you'll ever need to boost your website's exposure and performance.

Who This Book Is For

This book is ideal for marketers, editors, bloggers, online publishers, business owners, entrepreneurs, solopreneurs, freelancers, consultants, copywriters, and webmasters.

Because the SONAR Content Distribution Model™ is powerful and cost effective, it's also ideal for companies of any size—small, mid-size, Fortune 500, boutique firms, start-ups, home-based businesses, and info-publishers.

In a nutshell, this book is a "must have" for virtually anyone who wants to use the Web to make money for themselves, their company, or their clients. It's the only online marketing book you'll ever need.

How to Use This Book

This book is written with both newbie and experienced online marketers in mind. There's loads of helpful illustrations, comprehensive information, real-life examples, performance history, tips for success, and even a template for benchmarking.

Of course, most of the book stems from my near 20 years of marketing and editorial experience working for top publishers and Fortune 500 companies. I also share my insight as a thriving consultant and the creator of SONAR. In addition, I've included coveted business insights from some of the most respected publishers in their fields.

By the time you finish this book, you'll learn how to turn content into cash using the SONAR Content Distribution Model™. Using SONAR will help with increased website visibility, traffic, brand awareness, lead generation, subscriber bonding, industry credibility, and sales.

Conventions Used in This Book

As you read through this book, you'll note several special elements that present additional information and advice beyond what you find in the regular text.

Note

This is a note that presents some interesting information, even if it isn't wholly relevant to the discussion in the main text.

I THOUGHT OF SOMETHING ELSE

I use sidebars to dig a little deeper into the topic at hand. Some sidebars are used to explain something in more detail when doing so in the main body text would've been intrusive or distracting. Others offer material that truly is ancillary but important to your overall understanding. Don't skip the sidebars, as you'll find important information in them!

1

Content Rules!

Many online business models exist, including these three key types:

- *Pure retail sites that sell merchandise (anything from books to vitamins). These websites are product or service based, and the primary focus is e-commerce.*

- *Websites whose goal is advertising dollars—meaning they get their revenues from high-traffic and third-party advertisements. Examples of this are popular news-related or social media websites where the site itself isn't selling anything per se, but rather are parlaying their popularity and exposure into advertising opportunities.*

- *Websites that primarily focus on using great free content for both lead generation (email collection) and sales. In other words, online publishing or info-publishing websites. These sites initially use free content to bring in leads (subscribers) and then, throughout the sales funnel, cross-sell and up-sell a variety of paid info-products to subscribers, such as ebooks, DVDs, membership sites, and similar.*

This book focuses on the third type—the free online publisher. This publishing model is effective because it uses the universal foundation of providing great free content that the target audience finds useful, thereby generating interest and website traffic. In exchange, the publisher gets increased leads, revenue, and market buzz.

As you might guess, free content is content that is available without paying a cost to access it.

You can find such content on publishing or informational websites or in e-zines (e-newsletters), online articles, e-books, bonus reports, bulletins, and whitepapers. This is also content that is available in the public domain, which includes any works published in the Unites States before 1923 and content not covered by intellectual copyrights.

Just to be clear, in this book I am not talking about leveraging paid-for content, such as membership-based websites, paid newsletters (printed or electronic), paid e-books or reports, magazine subscriptions, and hard-cover or soft-cover books. What I *am* talking about is how to leverage free content (such as editorial and info-publishing products) to grow your business.

Nearly every website provides some sort of content. However, to use content as a way to generate leads and sales, you must become a bona fide online publisher.

Publishing content and information doesn't necessarily involve a lot of time, energy, or resources. If you're just starting out, you can put your toe in the water and publish timely e-alerts or e-bulletins. These alerts can be information that pertains to your industry and are what I call UVA: useful, valuable, and actionable for your reader. You don't have to commit to a distribution date, but you should target at least once per month to keep the lines of communication (and bonding!) open between you and your subscribers, or your audience will grow cold. However, it's important to note that if you don't commit to a consistent circulation date, there are potential consequences. It's more effective if you have a regular editorial schedule, as it helps your subscribers know when to expect your content. You want to consistently deliver content on the same day and time like clockwork. Once your subscribers start looking forward to receiving your content, you should see your click-thru rates improve. This will also encourage bonding and familiarity, thereby reducing attrition (opt-outs) and spam reports. Without this consistency, you run the risk of subscribers forgetting that they signed up (opted in) to receive your content and might inadvertently report you as spam as well as unsubscribe from your publication.

If you have a little more time or resources allocated to writing, you could publish a weekly or daily e-newsletter (known as an e-zine or e-letter). You need to solidify a list of prerequisites before you launch, however. Among these, you'll need to develop a template; decide on the layout, colors, and other aesthetics; create your editorial calendar; decide whether you will be the sole guru or whether you'll have expert contributors; pick an email service provider to send your email newsletter; and, of course, build your subscriber list.

MY 10 "MUST HAVES" FOR A GREAT FREE NEWSLETTER

1. The newsletter must be entertaining and engaging—in other words, a good read. It should also provide useful, valuable, and actionable content.

2. The content should be written informally, as if you're speaking to a friend who's across the table from you. It shouldn't be worded in academic or clinical language.

3. The content should have a Flesch–Kincaid readability scale level of sixth to eighth grade. You can find a free readability score checker at www.addedbytes.com/tools/readability-score/.

4. Keep in mind that the overall goal is to build a community of loyal readers. Building a strong community of readers helps your business increase its customer lifetime value (LTV), resulting in increased consumer loyalty, product sales, and referral business (word-of-mouth marketing).

5. Use the real estate in your free newsletter to cross-promote your products or your affiliate partners' products via text or banner ads. You can also include advertorial blurbs that tie into the actual article but link to related products via editorial notes. However, the editorial messages should outweigh the marketing messages. Keep your content-to-advertisement ratio to no more than 80:20 or 75:25. Each issue has the potential to bring in revenues, but you still are providing valuable content at no cost.

6. Offer a free bonus report or whitepaper to prospects as an incentive to sign up for the free subscription.

7. Tout your privacy and antispam policy on your website and in your newsletter, to help readers and prospects feel more secure about giving you their email address.

8. Remind readers at the top of your newsletter that they opted in to receive this information. For example: "You are getting this email because you subscribed to it on wwww.precisionmarketingmedia.com.html or www.musclemarketing.blogspot.com/, or because you are one of Wendy's clients, prospects, seminar/event attendees, or product buyers. You may unsubscribe below via SafeUnsubscribe if you no longer wish to receive our emails."

9. Have the options Forward to Friend, White List Us, and Cancel clearly available in your newsletter.

10. Include a "Syndicate Our Content" blurb at the bottom of each issue and on your website's newsletter archives page, to encourage web syndication and viral marketing. For example: "Like what you've read? Republish it for free and share the knowledge! Attention readers, publishers, editors, bloggers, marketers, and webmasters: *You may republish or syndicate my articles without charge.* The only thing I ask is that you keep the newsletter article or blog post exactly as it was written and formatted, with no changes. *You also must include full publication attribution and back-links* as indicated: "This information has been provided by www.musclemarketing.blogspot.com/ and Precision Marketing eNewsletter published by Wendy Montes de Oca, MBA. For more information or to sign up for a free subscription, visit www.precisionmarketingmedia.com/newslettersignup.html.""

Publishing websites have content, of course. It's their livelihood. These sites include news and newspaper sites, magazine sites, online periodicals, and similar sites. However, remember that blogs are also publishing sites—and there, the content is the message. If you have a blog or newsletter, you're already halfway there. You have the arsenal and just need to start syndicating your content on the Web.

A proven and powerful way to leverage content is to use the Customer Content Funnel. This model, shown in Figure 1.1, illustrates how you can use and repurpose content for prospecting (lead generation) and for sales. It also shows the varied price-point levels you can use to appeal to a variety of buyers.

> You have the arsenal and just need to start syndicating your content on the Web.

Customer Content Funnel

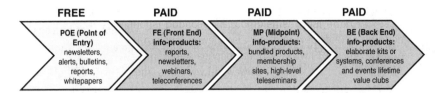

Figure 1.1   *Customer Content Funnel*

Hidden Places to Find Your Content

As a consultant, and even when working for top publishers, I often had to be a creative *and* strategic thinker. And while launching many start-up efforts, I also had to be aware of unnecessary costs—that is, if I needed content, I had to think of existing places to find it instead of hiring a writer to develop new content.

I made a list of all the potential places where I could find valuable content for my online syndication and marketing efforts:

- Old newsletter issues
- Old website articles or blog posts
- Old or outdated products
- Bonus materials (free reports)
- Teleseminars
- Webinars
- Interviews
- Event and conference audio or video transcripts
- Conference calls
- General website content

Old Newsletters, Articles, and Blog Posts

This is the first place to look for reusable content. Look for "evergreen" articles, in which the content of the article is still applicable today and will be for the foreseeable future. In other words, it has a long shelf life. Review the articles and remove or edit any references to a specific time or turn of events. Also look for newsworthy articles that have universal appeal to your target audience. "How to" and "Top 10" articles are always good to use. Other choice articles include forecasts, trends, breakthroughs, interviews with a known personality, contrarian or controversial viewpoints, or anything that ties into the reader's top emotional "hot buttons"— these can include vanity (as with anti-aging or being fit), greed (as with making money), fear, guilt, anger, exclusivity, or salvation.

People always want to gain health, time, popularity, wealth, advancement (socially or professionally), security or comfort, self-confidence, praise, and prestige. If your content touches on any of these elements, it will likely resonate with both universal and niche audiences.

Old or Outdated Products

Look through any old products you have. Info-products are the best—binders, e-books, reports, DVDs, or CDs. Start by product title and overall product objective, to see if the topic is relevant to your target reader. If so, review the actual content of the product, looking for content excerpts or snippets you can use to create new articles. You can also take excerpts from multiple products under the same theme if all the content flows and makes sense when you put it together in an article or a series of cliff-hanger articles. Finally, it's also important to make sure that the content you pick is timely and still holds value. You certainly don't want to pick outdated material or content that doesn't apply to the reader.

Bonus Materials

Many publishers pair free reports or whitepapers with their lead-generation efforts to bring in new subscribers. Apply the same slicing and dicing you're doing with your old products to your old bonus materials. Look for topics that will resonate with your target reader and seek out content that is engaging and timely. When you're doing article marketing, it's important to give enough beneficial information without giving away the whole caboodle. The idea is to pull in the reader with teasers (or useful information nuggets), but save the hard-core recommendations or serious data for cross-sell and up-sell opportunities.

Events: Teleseminars, Conferences, Webinars, and More

Just because the content isn't sitting in a neat, pretty book doesn't mean you can't leverage it. Many people speak at industry conferences, hold customer events, and conduct teleseminars and webinars. These can be free or paid events. However, don't overlook them because the content is video or audio based. For webinars and teleseminars, go through the PowerPoint or script files to see what bits of information you can use. For taped events, listen to the audio or watch the video. If you find something interesting, relevant, and timely, have the content transcribed into contextual format. You can then use the cleaned-up transcript in its entirety or focus on certain snippets for your marketing initiatives.

Interviews

Somewhere in your company archives, you might find an audio interview or Q&A session between the president or editor and a notable or relevant personality. These are great tools you can use in your article marketing efforts because they will certainly be interesting to your target reader and will have tremendous search engine value using the interviewer and interviewees names in your keyword tagging.

General Website Content

Finally, check the content on your website. Perhaps you'll find something useful in the "About Us" section. Maybe you have a frequently asked questions (FAQs) section on your site with some relevant questions to readers. Or maybe you have a Glossary or a press area of the site with information you can expand upon and turn into an article. Don't overlook what's right under your nose. Sometimes the most useful information is already online but hasn't been used to its full potential.

Sometimes the most useful information is already online but hasn't been used to its full potential.

2

Online Content Syndication: What You Need to Know

Online content syndication is a system or method in which online publishers republish articles, news items, press releases, blog posts, videos, or any other form of original material through various social media and Internet marketing channels.

You can syndicate your content in an automated way or manually. If you choose to automate it, setting up a Really Simple Syndication (RSS) or atom feed on your website achieves content syndication seamlessly. This involves doing some minor programming and incorporating website plug-ins. An RSS or atom feed enables users to get web feeds from your updated content, such as blog posts, newsletter articles, headlines, and more. Users download the application and then automatically receive their feeds in a specified format, usually XML. Simply put, when readers subscribe to your feed, they automatically receive each item that you publish. Most readers subscribe to multiple feeds, so each day they receive a variety of articles, blog posts, and other information from the various publishers they subscribe to.

With manual syndication, you (the publisher) would take editorial content (articles, for instance) and push it out to targeted online locations, such as networks, directories, or websites and blogs that allow for content submission. This tactic involves market research to see which sites are relevant for your target audience, as well as which sites will benefit from the content you're pushing out—in other words, websites or blogs where your content would fill an editorial void.

Perhaps you could share a unique viewpoint that a particular site doesn't cover yet. Or perhaps the site doesn't have content and needs an expert's voice to bring in traffic. Selecting your potential publishing partners' needs to be a targeted and specific process. Your potential publishing partners might be industry friends you already know, friendly competitors, or complete strangers. Relationship development and cultivation is key to long-term mutually beneficial arrangements that could lead to other business opportunities, such as cross-marketing, affiliate marketing, and joint ventures.

To start looking for potential, synergistic publishing partners, you first start by conducting searches for keywords that are similar to the name or category of your business, products offered, or target audience.

For example, if you want to manually distribute financial newsletter content and are looking for other sites on the Internet that might republish your articles, you can start by simply searching Google for terms such as "financial websites," "financial newsletters," "financial articles," or "submit financial content." The results that come up are your lead results—that is, possible venues for your editorial contributions.

You can then examine these results to see whether they have editorial relevance and opportunity to your specific needs. The more defined your search is, the more narrow your search results will be.

You can also use free online tools, such as Alexa and Compete, to get some ideas of which other websites could be worth contacting:

- **Alexa (www.alexa.com)**—Enter a competitor's website address or your own. A list of sites that the user also visits appears in the Related Links tab. For example, let's say you already have an arrangement with an online publisher such as EarlyToRise.com (ETR). If you enter www.earlytorise.com, Alexa returns www.selfgrowth.com and www.totalhealthbreakthroughs.com—both of which are relevant, synergistic websites to ETR's website visitors, as well as other potential publishing partners in the same vein as ETR that would be worth contacting.

- **Compete (www.compete.com)**—In the Site Profile section, enter either your website or a competitor's website; then, under Referral Analytics choose, Show Destination Sites. You'll see similar websites that visitors are frequenting, which again, are more potential publishing partners for you to contact. Note: This is not a free service. To access the Referral Analytics data, you need to subscribe to Compete's Pro Service for a nominal fee.

When you find some solid candidates to follow up with, simply call or email them (also known as cold contacting), explaining your credentials, relevance, content, and editorial objective. Your goal is to create another outlet in which your content will get "interest-free" exposure.

WHY WOULD I DO IT INTEREST FREE?

By "interest free," I simply mean that you acknowledge you will not receive any monetary compensation for the content. Instead, in exchange for your content, you'd like the other publisher to grant you an author byline (attribution) or editorial note immediately following your article that contains a short description of you and a back-link to your website. In addition to the obvious SEO benefits the back-linking will get you, the added exposure to another publisher's audience will help expand your overall market visibility, enforce your credibility as an expert, and encourage referral lead generation and website visits.

Whether you decide to syndicate your content manually or automatically via an RSS feed, you've made a wise decision for your business. Syndicating content has become increasingly important over the years and is a natural way for online publishers (especially those with little to no startup advertising budget) to create website traffic, create visibility, and aid in search engine marketing and optimization (SEM/SEO) efforts.

Content Syndication Networks

To syndicate content, you can also take advantage of content syndication networks (which I discuss in more detail in Chapter 6, "Learning and Leveraging the SONAR Content Distribution Model") that align themselves with publishers and act as an intermediary in disseminating publishers' content throughout the Web. Perhaps one of the most well-known content syndication sources in the world is the Associated Press (AP), which gathers news from news outlets around the world and distributes it to everyone subscribing to the AP. An online syndication network works in much the same way. Some examples of content syndication networks are www.synnd.com/ and www.contentsyndication.tiekinetix.com/.

With a content syndication network, a publisher provides content, and the syndicate distributes it to all members of the network. Typically, a fee is charged for the service. In some cases, there is no fee, but the syndicate might earn revenues from sponsorship ads embedded within the editorial content. So, for instance, if you're a publisher that contracts with a syndicate network to provide alternative health content, you will likely see related health ads alongside your content that the network is getting revenues for from a third-party advertiser. The one caveat with this is that if you choose to go this route, it's important to find out if you, the publisher, has a right to remove any ads that you feel could be jeopardizing to your editorial efforts, such as inappropriate or directly competitive ads. Some networks may even ask for a list of competitors or ad types that you might want suppressed (that is, turned off) around your content.

Using a content syndication network can be a viable solution for companies that truly want to extend their reach and have the financial resources to do so.

Content Aggregators

Simply put, a content aggregator is a site that gathers a specific kind of information from multiple sites. Some well-known examples are Google News and Yahoo! News. If you want Google News to carry your content, you must meet certain criteria. Typically, your website must be deemed "newsworthy," meaning that if you distribute a newsletter, it must be timely and must contain true editorial content, not self-promoting messages. In addition, you might need to have certain web pages already set up at the time you apply for consideration, including a newsletter archive (that archives issues in WordPress format), a page with a list of authors and editors (such as an "About Us" or staff page), and a "Contact Us" page. If you meet all the requirements, you simply submit an application and await a reply. For more information and submission criteria, visit www.google.com/support/news_pub/ or help.yahoo.com/l/us/yahoo/news/forms/submitsource.html.

The Art of Article (Content) Marketing

For many startup publishing companies, article marketing (or "content marketing") is a viable tactic to help create awareness about the business, build credibility for the author (as an expert), drive traffic to the company website, and help with search engine marketing and link-building efforts.

Article marketing is a little- to no-cost marketing tactic that doesn't take much time to implement. I help you refine and expand this technique when I discuss my SONAR Content Distribution Model™ in Chapter 6, in which article marketing is one piece of a more powerful puzzle. SONAR, as opposed to article marketing alone, is more strategic, comprehensive (multiple online channels), and casts a wider net.

Article marketing simply involves repurposing content—an article, blog post, or other editorial piece—for content syndication and republication by other, related publishing sites. The article itself should be relevant, beneficial, and useful to your target prospect (in other words, your ideal reader). To increase the appeal of an article, I prefer to use articles that cover industry hot buttons, a breakthrough, or something that's not widely known. Keep in mind that news syndicates carry a lot of articles, so yours needs to grab the reader's attention.

For optimal results, I recommend doing article marketing at least once per week—that is, uploading your repurposed articles to relevant article directories. This consistency enables you to incorporate it into your weekly routine, as well as keep a constant presence in the directory or directories you're submitting to, which increases your odds for website traffic, exposure, and reader bonding.

Content Syndication and Search Engines: Debunking the Duplicate Content Myth

I think there's a huge misunderstanding about how to distribute your content without hurting your website in the eyes of search engines.

After getting numerous questions from clients and reading various posts on blogs, there seems to be a common misunderstanding with regard to syndicating content that I would like to clear up. I get numerous questions from clients about syndicating content. The misconception is that by taking content and disseminating it around the Web on related, relevant websites or blogs, you adversely affect your website's organic search engine ranking (also known as search engine results page or "SERP") and integrity with major search engines, such as Google.

Just to be clear, content syndication is not the same as content farming or duplicate content—both of which will adversely affect your website.

> …content syndication is not the same as content farming or duplicate content…

 Note

Of course, I do not recommend link farming or content farming in any way. However, those methods are not what I'm talking about here, and is not usually what gets people confused about the duplicate content myth.

- **Content farming**—Google is often changing algorithms to offset unscrupulous websites that engage in industry no-no's such as "link farming," "content farming," and other frowned-upon practices that falsely boost website rankings in the eyes of the search engines. These sites typically abuse SEO tagging, have several irrelevant links going to and from their website, as well as have unrelated, unnecessary content linking to their main website and several other "gateway" pages around the Web. This is usually done in an effort to trick Google and other search engines into thinking the poor-quality website is actually of higher quality and more popular (search-worthy) than it really is.

- **Duplicate content**—If you create content, you should have the original content published on your website. However, you can repurpose it and strategically distribute it on the Web without hurting your SEO (search engine optimization) efforts with Google.

The key is to have the original article on your website and then use slightly modified versions of the article for syndication purposes uploaded to other websites or article directories—all linking back to your original content. For example, you could slightly modify the headline, intro or closing paragraph, and so on; or modify versions as excerpts instead of full articles, and somewhere in the body text include a link to the original source.

Algorithms are always changing, but typically Google and other search engines assign a higher ranking in organic search results to the original version of the content. Because Google represents the largest slice of the search engine pie, I'll focus on their current stance, according to industry blogs and Google's Webmaster Central.

In Google's view (see http://www.google.com/support/webmasters/bin/answer.py?answer=66359), "[...duplicate content generally refers to substantive blocks of content within or across domains that either completely match other content or are appreciably similar." What this means is that content is more hurtful for a site if it's posted in more than one place on the same domain (not via syndication on other websites, such as through online press releases, article directories, and so on).

For example, if you have two pages on your site with virtually the same content, Google likely notices this and ignores one of those web pages. Just one of these listings, not both, will appear in the organic search engine results.

Google determines that your pages are duplicated only if your page titles and meta descriptions are the same. So, make sure each web page on your site has unique, relevant tags with targeted keywords.

Google does mention on its Webmaster Central page to "syndicate carefully" stating, "If you syndicate your content on other sites, Google will always show the version we think is most appropriate for users in each given search, which may or may not be the version you'd prefer. However, it is helpful to ensure that each site on which your content is syndicated includes a link back to your original article...."

If you're concerned about web pages on your website and their text "printer-friendly version" hurting your website's ranking, simply block the search engines from spidering the print-friendly version using a robots.txt file. If you're not familiar with how to do this or need more information about acceptable website practices, I suggest checking out Google's Webmaster Central page at www.google.com/support/forum/p/Webmasters?hl=en. For a sample of steps you can take to proactively address duplicate content issues, visit www.google.com/support/webmasters/bin/answer.py?answer=66359.

The Article Directory: The Nucleolus of Your Web Content Marketing Efforts

Within article directories are members or "authors," and those authors can upload their original (not plagiarized) content for publication. After you open a free account and enter basic information about yourself, you can (within the directory's editorial guidelines) upload original content (see Figure 2.1). You can select related categories for the content and enter your headline, teaser, body copy, and keywords (or "tags") that will help web surfers find your article both within the directory network and on the Web itself (via organic search results), as shown in Figure 2.2.

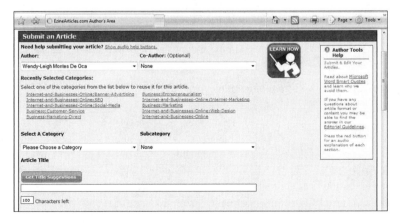

Figure 2.1   *Submitting an article for syndication is an easy task.*

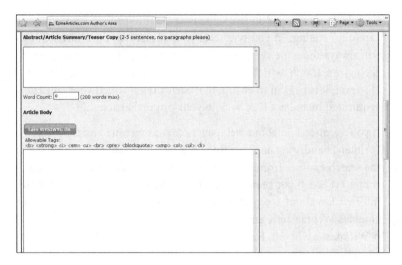

Figure 2.2   *Enter teaser copy and the article body here.*

You can also include your biography and website back-link in a custom signature (see Figure 2.3), and you can schedule the release of your articles (see Figure 2.4).

Figure 2.3   *Enter a custom biography, if you like.*

 Note

> The custom biography section is important, as it might be the only field
> that allows your website's back-link (to encourage website traffic). You can
> also enter your targeted keywords here to help users within the directory
> find your article, as well as help tie in with external keywords for your
> search engine marketing (SEM) efforts.

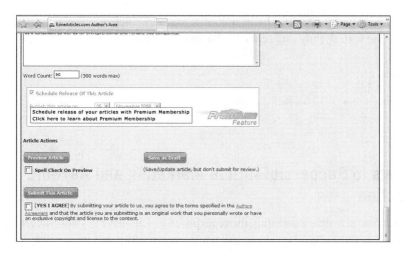

Figure 2.4 *Scheduling a release date for the article is easy. It's also important to spell check and agree to the directory's terms and conditions.*

The general rule of thumb in most article marketing directories is that the content cannot be blatantly self-promotional. Instead, the article must be pure editorial copy. In addition, many article directory sites forbid or limit the number of hyperlinks embedded within the content. For example, one of the most popular directories, EzineArticles.com, doesn't allow hyperlinks in the body copy, but it does allow them in the Author Signature/Resource Box. Make sure you read and follow the rules for each article directory accordingly.

After you submit your article, a member of the article directory's staff reviews it and then notifies you if it is approved. If it's not approved, the staff alerts you to edits that you need to make for publication. This review can take from one to five days. An established author (who has published many articles) or an author who has a premium membership gets expedited turnaround time.

For example, let's say you wrote a 500-word article and published it on your website. Your next step would be to make some repurposed versions of the primary content. You could do the following to create a repurposed version:

- Shorten the overall article or upload an excerpt that still maintains the integrity of the original article.

- Reorganize the content (making sure the content still flows and makes sense).

- Write new headlines and subheadlines.

- Write new transitional sentences between headings.

After you repurpose your article, upload it to several high-traffic article directories, each one with slightly different edits but overall the same article.

 Note

Remember, it's important to create a slightly different version of the article for each article directory to which you want to post your article.

Secrets to Successful Article Marketing and Keyword Selection

In successful article marketing, the repurposed articles have keyword-dense headlines and subheadings. It's also important to weave additional relevant keywords into the body copy.

Keywords or keyword phrases are simply words that are relevant to your content and to your target prospect. A keyword is a single word; a keyword phrase is a string of keywords. The goal is to use keywords or phrases that your ideal reader will likely search under but that are also relevant to the surrounding content. Relevancy is key!

Therefore, keyword selection is critical for your most significant web surfers to find your article, read it, and follow through to your website to read more of that great content.

Conducting initial keyword research and identifying your target audience is crucial in successful article marketing(as well as with my SONAR Content Distribution Model™, since article marketing is one of the cornerstones of the strategy. But I'll go into that more in Chapter 6).

> Conducting initial keyword research and identifying your target audience is crucial...

When it comes to selecting keywords to go with articles, some writers choose their keywords first and then write their article around those keywords. I like to think of my topic first and then work in my keywords so that the writing flows more organically. When I refine my final draft, I sprinkle in relevant keywords where necessary. Writing the article first and then choosing keywords ensures that your article is written for the "human" reader. Adding select keywords after the fact only enhances the content and optimizes it so that the search engines can "read" it (also known as indexing or spidering) better.

Before you get started with creating your content, it's important to ask yourself a few questions:

- Who is my target audience?

- What does my target audience want to read about? (That is, what is the topic?)

- What might my target prospect search under when looking for this topic?

When you start writing and repurposing your article with these questions in mind, you see that the primary keywords will naturally work their way into the content. Then, after your first draft, reread the content and pepper in any keywords that might be beneficial to the article.

Keep in mind that you don't want to repeat the same keywords throughout your article. Search engines look at this as "keyword stuffing," and it can actually hurt your search engine ranking. Don't be redundant—be creative. Think of relevant keywords and different variations of those keywords.

For example, let's say one of your primary keywords is "weight loss," your target audience is people wanting to lose weight, and your topic is healthy eating for better living.

Some variations of the phrase "weight loss" include the following:

Weight management

Weight reduction

Dieting

Shedding pounds

Lose weight

Healthy eating

Fat reduction

Calorie management

Body makeover

Getting slim

Losing inches

These are all words and phrases related to your primary keyword, but they're not the primary keyword repeated. These words should be weaved within your content as well as used as your search engine tags.

To find your relevant article keywords, start by making a list of your top 5–10 primary keywords (also known as root or core keywords). These are words that are relevant and based on your target audience, website, and content. Then, use a keyword search tool to see the actual global and domestic (local) search volume on those terms in both paid and organic search results.

Many keyword search tools exist. Most are free, but some are paid subscription services. These are among the most widely used search tools:

- www.keyworddiscovery.com/overture-keyword-suggestion-tool.html

- www.wordtracker.com/

- www.keyworddiscovery.com/search.html

My favorite keyword-suggestion tool – Google AdWords – is offered by search engine giant Google. I find this tool to be extremely easy to use, accurate, and comprehensive.

See https://adwords.google.com/select/KeywordToolExternal.

Google's keyword search tool enables the user to see the actual global and domestic (local) search volume on specified terms in paid search results, which also ties into the organic search results. The tool also suggest related keywords based on your specified query.

Figure 2.5 shows a keyword search, using "financial newsletter."

Figure 2.5   *Enter the primary keyword words that you are targeting.*

After you enter the keywords you are searching for, follow these steps:

1. Google shows results related to your terms, including the number of global monthly and local monthly searches (see Figures 2.6 and 2.7).

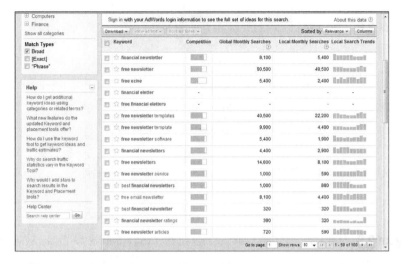

Figure 2.6   *Google returns an expanded list of related keywords.*

Figure 2.7   *Your keyword results will appear to download. This range can vary, but in this example, it is 100 keyword search ideas.*

2. The next step is to download the results into an .csv file for Excel (see Figures 2.8 and 2.9).

Figure 2.8 *Download the data. Leave this set to the default CSV format.*

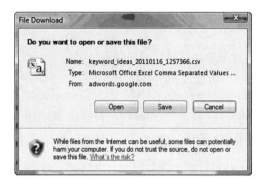

Figure 2.9 *Save the data in a spreadsheet so that you'll have it for future reference.*

3. After the raw data has been downloaded into your spreadsheet, sort and delete all columns except Keywords, Competition, Global, and Local (see Figures 2.10 and 2.11).

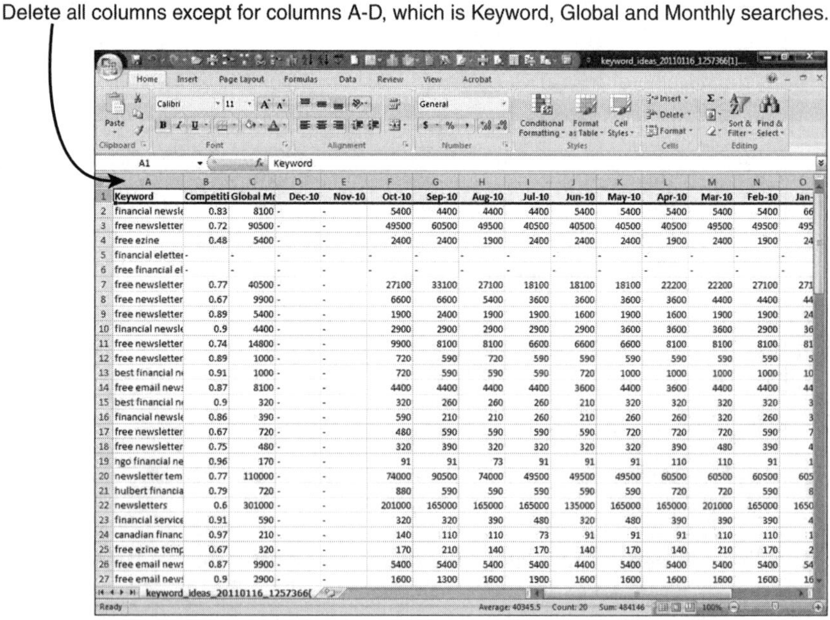

Delete all columns except for columns A-D, which is Keyword, Global and Monthly searches.

Figure 2.10 *Most of the raw data imported to Excel isn't needed.*

4. Next, sort the data in descending order. Sort the data by global or local searches based on the geographic region you're targeting (see Figure 2.11).

✉ *Note*

> Sorting by geographic region clearly segments the keywords by relevance and popularity (search volume). The key is to find the "search sweet spot"—that is, the keyword numerical results that are not too competitive (high) or too under-searched (low). Your goal is to pick approximately 10–15 primary keywords.

Figure 2.11   *Sort data by the number of monthly searches, in descending order (from most to least).*

5. Finally, review the list, add decimals to fields with numbers, and highlight the relevant keywords words that have modest search volume for clarity (see Figure 2.12).

	A	B	C	D	E	F
1	Keyword	Global Monthly Searches	Local Monthly Searches			
2	financial eletter	-	-			
3	free financial eletters	-	-			
4	stocks	3,350,000	2,240,000			
5	stock market	2,240,000	1,220,000			
6	personal finance	368,000	201,000			
7	newsletters	301,000	165,000			
8	stock picks	90,500	74,000			
9	newsletter templates	110,000	60,500			
10	stock investing	90,500	60,500			
11	free newsletter	90,500	49,500			
12	email newsletter	110,000	49,500			
13	newsletter ideas	18,100	12,100			
14	stock newsletter	18,100	12,100			
15	free newsletters	14,800	8,100			
16	newsletter sign up	22,200	8,100			
17	financial newsletter	8,100	5,400			
18	free email newsletters	9,900	5,400			
19	free email newsletter	8,100	4,400			
20	investment newsletter	6,600	4,400			
21	company newsletter	9,900	4,400			
22	online newsletters	5,400	3,600			
23	sample newsletters	4,400	3,600			
24	newsletters online	5,400	3,600			
25	financial newsletters	4,400	2,900			
26	newsletters templates	5,400	2,900			
27	kiplinger.com magazine	2,900	2,900			

Figure 2.12   *Highlight the most relevant keywords in your "search sweet spot."*

You might have keywords that have been searched as many as 1 million times or as few as 10. I like to pick related keywords and phrases in the range of 5,000 to around 75,000 in local search volume. If you're using the global search volume as your data reference point, I suggest narrowing the search range to perhaps 1,000–50,000 because the overall universe is much broader and more competitive (worldwide).

Choosing the Right Article Directory: The Importance of Rank and Relevance?

When it comes to article marketing, knowing where to disseminate your content is just as important as finding the content itself. Many article directories, social bookmarking sites, and user-generated content sites exist. However, the most important consideration is quality, not quantity. You want to upload your repurposed article to both high-traffic general directories and specialized directories pertaining to your niche.

For example, if your specialty is alternative health, the niche directories SelfGrowth.com, HealtheirTalk.com, and EHealthArticles.com might be relevant. You can find niche directories by doing a web search for terms such as "'top alternative health article directories." However, when you're trying to determine a directory's popularity, focus on the two Rs—rank and relevance:

> ...knowing where to disseminate your content is just as important as finding the content itself.

- **Rank**—Check the Alexa Page Rank of the article directory (a loose interpretation of a website's traffic or visits and popularity).

- **Relevance**—Upload your article to websites or directories that are relevant (synergistic) to your content and overall website.

Rank and relevance are important because your articles are back-linked from the directory in which they are hosted to your site. Articles also are back-linked to your site from any location where your article is republished (or syndicated), which can be other third-party websites or blogs. This back-link, or "link juice," aids in your search engine optimization efforts and is one of the variables that determines your placement in the organic search results. Irrelevant or unrelated websites that link back to your site can negatively affect your organic search rank. Back-links from high-traffic, popular sites have a positive impact on your search rank.

Article directories enable members' submissions of original content to be published in their directories and then segmented under various topics and keywords. This appears both within the directory and in organic search results under specific keywords, thereby generating traffic to the source article. The publication of the article also helps build awareness of and credibility for the author as an expert in a specific topic area.

Table 2.1 shows the top 15 article directories by Alexa Page Rank.

Table 2.1   Top 15 Article Directories by Alexa Page Rank

	Directory Name	Alexa Traffic Rank
1.	ezinearticles.com	114
2.	articlesbase.com	337
3.	suite101.com	651
4.	buzzle.com	656
5.	helium.com	1,167
6.	goarticles.com	1,650
7.	articlesnatch.com	1,861
8.	articlealley.com	2,110
9.	articledashboard.com	3,186
10.	selfgrowth.com/articles.html	3,454
11.	bukisa.com	3,762
12.	ideamarketers.com	4,286
13.	amazines.com	4,759
14.	isnare.com	5,241
15.	searchwarp.com	5,563

Source: www.vretoolbar.com/articles/directories.php

Other notable sites not listed in the table include American Chronicle and Articles Factory.

TOP SIX MOST POPULAR SOCIAL BOOKMARKING WEBSITES, BY PAGE RANK

Social bookmarking sites help users in the network share content and websites based on what's popular among readers with like-minded interests. This generates traffic to the original content source page and also viral buzz. Table 2.2 shows the six most popular social bookmarking websites.

Table 2.2   Six Most Popular Social Bookmarking Websites

	Site	Alexa Traffic Rank
1.	Yahoo! Buzz	3
2.	Twitter	9
3.	Digg	116
4.	StumpleUpon	172
5.	Reddit	247
6.	Delicious	269

To Outsource or Not to Outsource...That Is the Question!

I often get asked whether it's worth outsourcing article marketing across the globe to inexpensive writers in countries such as Pakistan, India, and the Philippines, who might typically charge as little as $5 an article.

My opinion is that if you have the resources to pay someone to do the work for you, it's worth a test. However, it's important to keep in mind that foreign writers (who use English as their second language) might be more prone to grammatical, spelling, or usage mistakes. They might also be unfamiliar with certain trade speak, jargon, slang terms, or other technical nuisances that could require extra rounds of editorial review.

Also, if you do outsource the work—whether it's domestic or international—make sure your vendor understands these key items:

- Who you're writing to (your target audience)
- How to use your top keywords in the content
- The need to keep your article friendly to both search engines and human readers

I highly recommend providing your vendor with some editorial guidelines that clearly illustrate these points.

3

The Power of Search: Understanding Search Engine Optimization for More Effective Content-Based Marketing Efforts

When deploying any online marketing tactic—especially ones that use content as a driving force, such as article marketing, and more importantly, the SONAR Content Distribution Model™ (which I'll explain more about in Chapters 6 and 7)—it's paramount to first understand how search engines work and what they do and don't like. Having this fundamental knowledge will help enhance overall performance. As I mentioned in Chapter 2, search engine algorithms are changing all the time, but a few search engine optimization (SEO) fundamentals always seem to remain the same.

Keyword Density

Search engines spider (or "index") pages from top to bottom. When putting together the content on your page, it's important to make the top of the page more keyword rich than the bottom. I like to think of an inverted pyramid: The top of the page, such as the headline, subheading, and introductory paragraph, should have the most relevant keywords. As you move down the page, the keywords narrow down.

Redundancy

Search engines view repetition of keywords as "keyword stuffing." Instead of repeating the same term, which also doesn't work well for the human reader, it's best to think of alternate variations of a term. For example, if your keyword is *antiaging*, alternative words might include *longevity, youth, aging backwards, reverse aging, looking younger, skin rejuvenation*, and *aging well*.

Tagging

On your website, you can take a few steps to aid your search engine optimization efforts (SEO). SEO is the term used for improving your organic (a.k.a. natural) search results. This can be done by incorporating keywords into your content and tags, to help search engines quickly and easily index your web pages. Tags are the behind-the-scenes codes that human eyes don't necessarily see but that the search engines do.

 Note

It's important to note that anyone can view their website's tags using the following directions, but unless you're experienced in making tag changes to your website, it's best to ask your webmaster or website programmer to implement any such changes that might be needed.

However, if you're interested in seeing what your current tags look like or how to find them, follow these instructions:

1. Open a web browser, such as Internet Explorer, Firefox, or Safari, and navigate to any site for which you want to see the metadata.

2. Select View from the top navigation bar.

3. A drop-down window appears; select Source (see Figure 3.1).

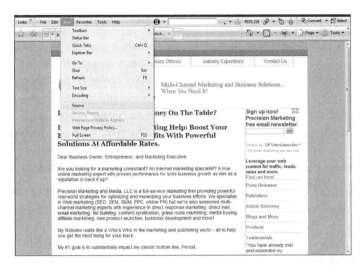

Figure 3.1   *In the Internet Explorer browser, Select Source from the View menu.*

 Note

Depending on your security settings, web browser, or the version of Windows your system may be operating on, you might see a warning message asking if you want to allow this action. Select Allow.

4. A file launches showing the HTML code (see Figure 3.2) and tags the search engine's index.

Figure 3.2   *You can view all meta information, including title tag, meta description, and meta keywords.*

You can find the following information in this useful file:

- **Title tag**—The title tag is the description that appears in the title bar at the top of your computer screen located above the search browser window. Both search engines *and* human visitors can read this. Therefore, the title tag should make sense to both people and search engines. The title should be keyword rich, different for each page of your website, and related to the page's overall content. The goal is to keep the total character count at less than 65 and to make each word be relevant. However, avoid repeating any one word more than four times.

- **Meta tags**—These are unique, relevant keywords that your ideal prospect will likely search for. Meta tags are behind the scenes, are seen only by the search engines, and are used to index the page in the search engine's database. As with the title tag, meta tags should be related to the web page's content. Ideally, you want a maximum of 25 keywords, with 25% to 50% of those keywords being your primary (root or core) keywords—these are the ones that reflect your overall business message and target audience search.

- **Meta keywords**—Meta keywords are the keywords or keyword phrases that appear most often on your page. As the other tags, keywords should be relevant and unique (not repetitive). Your most important keywords should be at the top of your list; then work your way down. These are the primary words related to your content, as well as would appeal to your target audience. Different blogs say different things as far as word count; I tend to lean toward what industry staple SEOLogic suggests, and that's 10–15 keywords or phrases.

- **Meta description**—The meta description is what readers see in the organic search listing results also known as search engine results pages (SERPs). This not only has to be keyword rich for search engines to find, but it also should make sense to the human reader. This is what your target audience will see when doing organic searches, and who the description is written for will prompt the click-through rate. The maximum character count is approximately 250. The meta description should also be unique for each page of your website and should relate to its overall content.

- **Alt tags**—Alt tags are keyword-rich tags for the relevant images (photos or graphic) on your web page. These often get overlooked when tagging is being done. When possible, it's a best practice to label the images with relevant keywords that relate to the image and the surrounding text. To see if your website images are tagged correctly, simply move your mouse across the image and read the text in the small text box that appears over the image.

- **Takeaways**—Be sure to consider relevance, keyword density, and specificity. All these elements are critical to your SEO tagging. Because search engine algorithms and website usage behaviors, which you can view via your site's analytics, are dynamic (capable of change), it's best to review your tags and site content every three to six months and make adjustments as necessary. At the very least, review your tags when significant changes to the site's content occurs, such as the addition of new web pages. Subsequently, make sure your webmaster updates your sitemap and submits it to the major search engines whenever new web pages are added to your site.

As a business owner, marketer, or publisher, you certainly don't have to know the nitty-gritty details of how to change your website's tags. As I mentioned earlier, that's best left for the experts: webmasters and web programmers. However, knowledge is power. It certainly doesn't hurt to know a little bit about how tagging works on your own site, as well as your clients' sites and your company's sites. If you ever find yourself working with an outside SEO agency, understanding the basics will help you cross-check and verify the work being performed. Knowing how and where to find this information will only help you understand online marketing and the SONAR Content Distribution Model™ better—and ultimately, give you more control and insight to help boost overall web performance.

Other SEO Secrets

With content marketing and SONAR in general (which I'll go into in Chapter 6), the fundamental strategy of leveraging your content on the Web, as well as your website, is relying heavily on the content itself, the search engines, and search engine optimization (SEO) techniques. For all of this to be effective, it's best to complement your content marketing or SONAR efforts with correctly implemented SEO and industry best practices.

So, in addition to the tagging basics I just covered, here are some additional tricks of the trade that can further optimize your website's content to achieve optimal performance with your content marketing and SONAR initiatives:

- Add H1 tags (header tags) in your body content to your web pages, to identify titles for search engine spiders.
- Emphasize keywords with bold, underline, or italic.

- Categorize keywords to relevant and related groupings (such as on a newsletter archives page, where content can be sorted by date, author, or topic).

- Engage in relevant link-building efforts.

- Incorporate intrasite links between relevant web pages.

- Add a site map to your website (similar to a table of contents, to help search engines index the site more quickly).

- Add keyword-rich content pages, such as a glossary and FAQ.

SEO for PDFs: Make Your PDFs Search Engine Friendly

A PDF is a Portable Document File created by Adobe Systems. It's simply a file that you can create in one application (such as PowerPoint, Word, Excel, or HTML) that contains text, images, drawings, and more, but it can be viewed by virtually anyone with Acrobat Reader.

Most people like to upload documents (especially important content-rich documents like press releases, articles, interviews, transcripts, and similar) in PDF format to their website for its universal access, ability to maintain document integrity either viewed onscreen or printed, and security features (files can be protected by making them read-only, so readers can't add to, change, or cut, copy, or paste material from them).

Because these types of documents play an important role in content marketing—and in the bigger scheme of things, the SONAR Content Distribution Model™—I want to make sure it's crystal clear how search engines index PDFs.

There's a misconception out there that search engines don't read (index) PDFs. They do. Of course, HTML pages are faster to index than a PDF, but PDFs can be indexed. The trick is to know how to set up the PDF to make sure you get maximum pick-up by the search engines.

Follow these top five tips to optimize the PDFs on your website for search engines:

1. Make sure each PDF file is text based and has the correct document properties set up. When the search engines index (or spider) a PDF, they extrapolate the text from the information fields within the PDF. That means the metadata and keywords you choose for these fields are critical. The important fields are the author, document title, description, file size, and modification date.

2. Remember to tag the PDF and use anchor text and links within the file. The same SEO best practices for websites apply to PDFs. In addition, make sure your links aren't buried deep within the PDF file. Have them at the root level, easy for search engines to find.

3. If you have a large PDF file, consider breaking it into smaller relevant groups, sections, chapters, and so on. Tag these sections accordingly with accurate, relevant keywords. This works not only for human readers, but also for search engines—as I mentioned, it takes longer to spider a PDF than HTML.

4. Check the PDF file format version number, and make sure search engines can read it. Typically, you want to use Acrobat 5/Adobe XMP (PDF V. 1.4 or 1.5).

5. Finally, make sure the reading order in your PDF is logical and flows. Again, this is user-friendly for humans and search engines. However, from a search engine perspective, your reading order gives you an idea of what will be displayed in organic search results. To do this, first open your PDF and select Advanced, Accessibility, Add Tags to Document. Then select Advanced, Accessibility, Touch Up Reading Order. This displays the reading order of the PDF.

If you have PDFs on your site already, it's a good idea to review them, to make sure they were originally set up correctly for search engines. Don't let your PDF content get overlooked—optimize it today![1]

Don't let your PDF content get overlooked—optimize it today!

1 Source: http://musclemarketing.blogspot.com/2009/06/seo-for-pdfsheres-what-you-need-to-know.html

FREE WEB CONTENT TAGGING TOOLS

The Web has many effective free tools to help you with your search engine optimization and tagging efforts. I like to use these:

- **Back-link checkers**—See who has linked back to you and who has syndicated your content:
  - www.backlinkwatch.com/index.php
  - www.iwebtool.com/backlink_checker
  - www.build-reciprocal-links.com/backlink_checker_tool.html
  - http://seopro.com.au/free-seo-tools/link-checker/
- **Keyword search tools**—Search for keyword ideas and volume:
  - www.keycompete.com
  - https://adwords.google.com/select/KeywordToolExternal
  - www.keyworddiscovery.com/search.html
  - www.vretoolbar.com/keywords/
- **Meta tag tools**—Generate tag ideas:
  - http://tools.seobook.com/meta-medic/
  - www.seologic.com/webmaster-tools/meta-tag-generator.php
  - www.seocentro.com/tools/search-engines/metatag-analyzer.html
- **Keyword density checker tool**—Check the density of your web pages:
  - www.iwebtool.com/keyword_density
  - http://tools.seobook.com/general/keyword-density/

4

What Came First: The Guerrilla or the Web?

According to Wikipedia.com, Web 2.0 is the commonly used term to describe various social media applications that help make the Internet more interactive and enhance the user experience.

Now, just because the Web 2.0 term was coined only a few years ago and social media marketing is all the current rage doesn't mean that these are new online marketing strategies.

More than a decade ago, I was already developing tactics that in today's terms would be viewed as social marketing and Web 2.0. These tactics involved visiting targeted chat rooms, forums, and message boards to interact with members and see what was on their minds. I also used these platforms to conduct market research, get ideas for new product development, and engage in prospecting efforts.

Note

> By "prospecting efforts," I mean copying and pasting links to relevant content about my employer's company as an FYI for forum members. I did this in the hopes that those members would be curious and click through to read more—and eventually end up as customers of my company.

In other words, my ultimate goal was to engage with the prospect—to develop some sort of social, interactive relationship with the members of those targeted chat rooms, forums, and message boards, which would generate website traffic, and, ultimately, sales.

Back then, Facebook, Twitter, and other popular social networking and bookmarking sites didn't exist. However, there *were* social communities—hubs of like-minded people who gathered in forums, chat rooms, or online message boards to talk about and share common interests. Even better, these locations were untapped resources—prime real estate—for turning strangers into friends. You see, 10 years ago, not many marketers were infiltrating these platforms for promotional purposes. Most were focusing their efforts on traditional direct mail or print advertising. Direct mail was the marketing method of choice, and it was making people money. So, many marketers and publishers had the notion, "If it ain't broke, don't fix it." As a result, the Web was being underutilized. If any online efforts *were* being done, it was by mavericks dabbling in banner ads or implementing search engine optimization.

The "social frontier" had yet to be exploited. However, some marketers, including myself, had come from organizations that encouraged and embraced the Web as a marketing tool to be tested and explored. We saw early on the true potential of the Internet and social-type platforms, and we had to slowly try to pitch this as a viable marketing channel to the die-hard direct mailers in the industry.

Looking back, I didn't call the online, interactive, social efforts I deployed "Web 2.0"—I called them "guerrilla marketing" because they were covert in nature. Every time I engaged with members in the chat rooms or forums for marketing purposes, I felt as if I was going on a stealth mission. In other words, I believe the origin of what is considered today's social marketing initiatives stems from guerrilla marketing. Let me explain....

"Guerrilla marketing" is a term that was first used by Jay Conrad Levinson in his 1984 book of the same name. To me, guerrilla marketing is similar to Web 2.0 (interactive, social) tactics. How? The marketer is looking for innovative, strategic, creative, low-cost, and, quite simply, nontraditional ways to reach his target prospect. This can be achieved by crafting various marketing, promotional, and public relations messages.

To really engage in this medium and leverage it to the fullest potential, it's important to be a creative *and* strategic thinker. That means you need to market smarter, not harder, and tap into your imagination and knowledge. There's an art to this kind of marketing—and it's not a one-hit wonder. You won't see overnight success; it takes time and resources.

Many companies often hire entry-level marketers or part-time college students to handle guerrilla marketing efforts. Some companies may even have members of their in-house marketing team spend time on this between more pressing matters. That was my case. During my off hours—either before work, during lunch, or after work—I went online and met up with my Internet "friends." I was testing out this exciting tactic on my own time, as a fellow member of the forum—not as a company employee. And I just happened to be sharing useful knowledge

> ...you need to market smarter, not harder, and tap into your imagination and knowledge.

about a great company (which I worked for) that I truly believed in. The forum messages were useful, relevant, and targeted. Truth be told, I just helped lead the proverbial horse to the water. The forum members (my "friends") had complete control over whether they were going to drink.

Around this same time, marketing legend Seth Godin was preaching about establishing a relationship based on "friendship" in his profound book, *Permission Marketing: Turning Strangers into Friends, and Friends into Customers.* I had read this book back in 1999, and it was professionally life changing. I was inspired with several ideas on how to leverage email and the Web for the ultimate in online business success.

In a nutshell, permission marketing is the opposite of interruption marketing—you know, those wonderful telemarketing phone calls that always seem to happen at an inopportune time, such as during dinner or right after you put your two-year-old child to sleep.

- Interruption marketing comes into your space unannounced—a cold call or an unsolicited stranger. It interrupts your moment with a marketing message and usually results in less-than-mediocre results.

- Permission marketing, however, is at the other end of the spectrum. It is relationship (socially) based. The idea is to turn a stranger into a friend, a friend into a customer, and then a customer into an advocate. The goal is to establish, build, and cultivate a relationship with your potential customers, thereby getting them to opt in to your messages— meaning that they are actually agreeing to receive your marketing messages. This opens the door to a plethora of marketing possibilities.

It can create brand loyalty, customer referrals, and multi-buyers (customers that buy repeatedly as well as purchase multiple price points/ products), as well as increase the lifetime value of your customers. This is exactly what I was doing with my guerrilla marketing, and it does take a certain amount of tact, experience, and finesses to deploy. There are rules of engagement.[1]

EMAIL COMPLIANCE

It's important whenever discussing Web and email marketing as well as opt-in policies to make sure you are complying with industry best practices, as well as federal anti-spam laws.

For more information, see the Direct Marketing Association's Council for Responsible E-Mail report: *E-Mail Delivery Best Practices for Marketers and List Owners* (www.the-dma.org/antispam/EmailBPFINAL.pdf).

To get familiar with the Federal Government's antispam law, better known as the CAN-SPAM Act of 2003, see http://business.ftc.gov/documents/bus61-can-spam-act-Compliance-Guide-for-Business.

Guerrilla Marketing and Social Media: The Rules of Engagement

As I mentioned earlier, in 2000, social marketing through chat rooms and forums wasn't overly popular, but savvy marketers were doing it as a part of their guerrilla marketing efforts.

Looking back, I think the best way to describe it was its similarity to the Wild West. This was before anti-spam laws—and before many marketing best practices were being communicated. There really weren't any rules, per se. Of course, reputable marketers didn't want to break any laws. Mostly what guided us were our own morals and ethics.

That was then—this is now. Today, social media marketing is huge. It's common practice to establish relationships with members of networks, communities, forums, blogs, chat rooms, and message boards. Furthermore, websites and publishers are encouraging reader interaction and participation.

1. What Is Guerrilla Marketing Anyway?, Al Lautenslager,
   http://www.entrepreneur.com/marketing/guerillamarketing/article193490.html.

And that encouraged reader participation is cultivating some of the fastest-growing marketing tactics online today. Posting on blogs and forums can be a powerful way to increase your market presence, further your SEO efforts, and drive traffic to your website.

Social sites are booming, and so are the efforts to tap into this rich and robust channel.

According to articles on Royal Pingdom, TechCrunch, and Wikipedia, these communities are growing exponentially—and that's only going to continue. Consider these online stats:

- 126 million blogs (as tracked by BlogPulse), as of December 2009
- 190 million people on Twitter, as of June 2010
- 500 million on Facebook, as of July 2010
- 75 million on LinkedIn, as of August 2010
- Over 15 million articles on Wikipedia, as of July 2010
- More than 2 billion views on YouTube each day, as of July 2010

Also take a look at these figures, according to an article in *USA Today* citing statistics from Forrester Research:

- Out of 1,217 business decision makers surveyed in 2008–2009, 95% use some form of social media.
- Fifty-three percent of more than the 300 marketers surveyed plan to increase social marketing budgets in 2009–2010.

In addition, SocialMediaExaminer.com released this recent data after surveying 1,898 people (98% of whom were business owners or employees):

- Nine out of 10 marketers, or 91%, use social media.
- Twenty-two percent just started using social media marketing, 43% have used it for a few months, 31% have used it for a few years, and only 3% have no experience in it.
- Fifty-six percent of marketers use social media marketing tactics for more than 6 hours per week; 30% use it for more than 11 hours per week.

10 Rules of Social Marketing (Guerrilla) Etiquette

As the social media landscape grows with mainstream and niche sites, so will the innovative ways to get marketing messages to members of these social media sites.

However, before you starting posting away with your guerrilla marketing tactics, it's good to keep in mind my 10 rules of social marketing etiquette:

1. **Be aware.** Know each social media community's law of the land. Each network, forum, blog, chat room, and bulletin board has its own set of rules that you are required to abide by as a member. Read the rules and stick to them. If the site has a specific area for promotional or marketing messages, keep your posts of this nature restricted to those areas. If rules dictate what type of messages are allowed (such as no overtly self-serving, defamatory, illegal, elicit, or pornographic material), follow the rules. Any deviation will prompt a warning by the site's moderator or a ban from the site.

2. **Be active.** Don't just go in a few times and hit members with your marketing message. Get involved. Participate in discussions. Interact with members. Read and respond to engaging posts with no hidden agenda.

3. **Be relevant.** Make sure you're posting in areas of the site that are relevant to the topic you're discussing. Many forums have segmented sub-areas by category and interest level. This helps the members easily find the topics they're interested in and keeps you from muddying the waters in unrelated areas of the site.

4. **Be genuine.** Let the conversations flow organically. Contribute real, thought-provoking comments that members will find interesting.

5. **Be useful.** As a member, your goal is to participate in intelligent, useful discussions. Make sure you're adding value to the site in some way. Your comments should also be valuable to the reader and not random posts. Nothing gets under members' skin more than messages that appear to be blatant spam.

> Contribute real, thought-provoking comments...

6. **Be subtle.** Don't overlink. Many marketers embed their entire message with URLs to whatever page they're trying to drive traffic to. Less is more here. Some sites even have rules about not allowing links in the body copy of a post, but keeping them only in the auto signature field where your username is. Links should be relevant to the post (such as a great article that you want to share with members—then enclose the link so they can read for themselves). Use links sparingly.

7. **Be balanced.** Mix up your messages. Don't just go into a site and start spamming away with your marketing messages. Go in. Hang out for a few weeks. Get to really know the members and the site. See which areas of the site have topics and discussions that vibe with you. Mix up

your posts. Find balance with the editorial and marketing messages you're posting. The idea is to provide value and engage. If you overmarket, it will be transparent, and you'll be labeled a "shill." That will affect your credibility with other members.

8. **Be informative.** Don't limit your article uploads or links to your own publication. Be aware of what's happening in your area of interest. Be able to have intelligent discussions about different news, events, and publications under your subject matter. If you see other related articles that you think members would find interesting—even material from other publishers—share the knowledge. After all, that's ultimately what social media is about.

9. **Be personable.** Develop relationships with the community on both a "friend" and an expert level for your area of specialty. Let your personality and credentials shine through with the information you share. Offer free expert advice. Share funny stories. Have witty discussions. Start to truly develop a memorable presence and bond with the community.

10. **Be respectful.** Don't spam your fellow members. Many social communities (such as Facebook and LinkedIn) post user email addresses on their Profile page. This leads to a flurry of unsolicited emails to the unsuspecting user from social networking barracudas that use this personal information for their own self-serving purposes. Remember, just because an email is posted on a user's profile page doesn't mean that person opted in to receive solicitations, promotions, or similar email communications. Sending unwanted and unsolicited emails is spam, plain and simple. Don't exploit community members' personal information.

Social Marketing Success Secrets

Social (guerrilla) marketing can be fun, can increase awareness, and can drive website traffic. You just need to know a few key elements to help monetize the efforts and best leverage the interactive relationship you're engaging in. But first, I'd like to explain the flow of information with social media marketing versus other forms of online marketing:

With social media marketing, the messages you're posting are drawing your friends, followers, and fans (a.k.a. the Triple Fs) into your profile or home page. This marketing distribution is passive, and the profile traffic is organic. Traffic visits are uncontrolled; the marketer/publisher solely relies on the reader responding to a post. What's more, the metrics, although somewhat quantifiable (see Chapter 8, "SONAR in Action: Results and Analytics"), are mostly based on assumptions.

The opposite is something like email marketing, which is a form of direct-response marketing. An email message is sent out to the recipient. This is a more targeted and aggressive approach because your message is going directly to someone's individual email box, where they've opted to receive your communications; you're not relying on the reader to stumble upon your profile or home page post. Results are easily tracked and measured, and the marketer/publisher can control distribution.

Now, what I'm about to say might raise some eyebrows, as social media marketing has become the new shiny thing many self-proclaimed Internet marketing gurus are raging about. And they may even argue that by friending or following someone, you've sort of opted in to receive the authors' messages that are being posted on your profile page, wall, or home page. I disagree.

Not everyone will be a "profile stalker"—that is, visiting someone else's profile page on a daily basis. And most home page posts will be lost among all the other friend and follower noise on the page.

In addition, accepting someone's friend invitation certainly doesn't give that person permission to send promotional-type communications to a personal email address (which, by the way, is visible information on some social media profile pages). As I mentioned earlier, unsolicited emails that a user hasn't opted in to receive are spam—no ifs, ands, or buts.

Social networking has become very popular, and community members often follow hundreds or thousands of people. Checking *your* profile page frequently or singling out *your* posts on a home page filled with many other messages is realistically unreliable, even for the most loyal of followers.

> ...unsolicited emails that a user hasn't opted in to receive are spam—no ifs, ands, or buts.

With email marketing, you're sending a direct message to your recipients. Sure, you're competing with other messages in their email inbox, but chances are, if you have a good subject line, your email will be seen and read—way better odds than a random profile or home page visit.

I mention this because although many people get excited when they see they have 500 friends or 1,000 followers, I believe it plays more to one's ego than anything else. For psychological reasons, we all want to have friends, fans, and followers—we want to feel popular, wanted, and liked.

Although there is value in creating a loyal community of like-minded Triple Fs, you still don't have a direct opted-in line of communication to them (via an email address), which makes the Triple Fs somewhat harder to monetize than free e-zine subscribers. Subscribers *are* people who've given permission to receive your communications, such as e-zine issues and direct email messages.

Subscribers have more of a vested interest in the relationship than the Triple Fs. After all, they have voluntarily given you personal information: their email address. And in the publishing industry, email addresses are one of the most important things one can get from a person, aside from a mailing address. You see, the email address is the foundation of your list, your community, and your lead-generation efforts.

This gives you leverage when coordinating joint ventures (JVs), affiliate marketing, and editorial deals with other publishers. This also gives you a direct, personal line of communication with the reader for special, targeted bonding and sales messages.

Email addresses are names that can be added into your sales funnel for direct email marketing efforts, which ultimately will help you turn a subscriber into a paying customer at a more expedited rate than through social media marketing.

Can a Triple F be converted into a paying customer without being a subscriber or receiving direct email messages?

Sure, but it's harder to bond with someone when the marketing messages are limited, passive, in public view, and reliant on the prospect to come to you (instead of you sending your message to them).

On some social media platforms, you're also dealing with limitations that can affect the potency of the message, such as maximum character counts. This dilutes the effectiveness of your overall marketing message and performance results.

I advise clients to use social marketing as a tool to assist with, and complement, their other online marketing efforts, not to put all their eggs in one basket and completely rely on social media marketing (SMM) just because it's popular or everyone seems to be doing it. As with any marketing tactic, in the end, it has to make sense for your business.

But you can take some steps to help maximize your returns with social media marketing. Incorporating the following tactics and being aware of the challenges you may come across helps you get the most of your social marketing efforts, to grow your business now and down the road. The following are some tips for getting the most from your SMM efforts.

Relationship Building and Bonding

The whole purpose of social media marketing is to connect your business with like-minded individuals with a common interest, and for your company to be part of a network or community. You have the ability to be a friend and guru. People friend, follow, or fan someone for a psychological reason: They feel like they're getting one step closer to their subject of interest, guru, celebrity, or idol. They also feel that they're getting the real deal, the inside scoop, and unedited, raw comments straight from the horse's mouth.

So, your goal should be to post engaging and somewhat personal messages for your "Triple F's": friends, followers, or fans. Don't bombard them with links to promotions or newsletters. In short, don't spam them with marketing. Mix it up a bit and ask thought-provoking questions. Post insightful comments and interesting nuggets of information. Engage in group discussions and witty conversations.

Engage in a One-on-One Dialogue

Exchange comments about family, sports, weather, jokes, or other areas of interest. Convey birthday wishes. Get to know your Triple F's on a personal level. With social media marketing, it's all about relationship cultivation and interaction. Engage with them and aim for open communication and two-way communication.

People also feel extra special through direct dialogue. Depending on how many Triple F's you have, pick a few random names and send them a direct message through the social media platform. For instance, Facebook offers email messaging (but remember not to send promotional messages through this venue, since it's a turn-off).

I also encourage you to upload semipersonal pictures to help "humanize" yourself—to be relatable. You want your Triple F's to look at you as a guru and a friend, not just as someone marketing at them. This will help you stand out in a sea of other people your Triple F's are following. That's what will keep visitors coming back to your website for other products or to sign up for your free newsletter.

Branding and Free Advertising

Incorporate your brand (image, logo, tag line) or promotional messages either in the background of your social media profile page or in text or banner ads on your social media profile page. Make the text ad or banner ad eye-catching, and link to your website home page, squeeze page (name-collection page), or promotional landing page. The landing page for the link in your ad should be determined by your goal and overall message.

Facebook has areas on individual pages (as opposed to fan pages) that could be used for advertising or promotional, such as text boxes, the Notes tab, Links, and Profile Badge. On fan or company pages, you can also upload 200×520 pixel vertical banner ads instead of a profile picture, for added advertising benefits. You can hyperlink the ad to your website, squeeze page, or wherever.

Note

Twitter also allows some advertising personalization via the Settings, Profile, and Design tabs.

Conversion

Remember, although you have links to your Triple F's profile pages, you don't have opted-in, direct email addresses. In other words, you don't have permission to send them promotional or editorial communications. To help remedy this, I typically put together a social media conversion plan, which is a strategic plan to encourage your company's Triple F's to sign up for your newsletter, moving them to subscriber status. After you have permission to send a newsletter to your Triple F's, you have

> ...your goal is to bridge the gap between friend/ follower/fan and customer.

implemented what's known as permission marketing. From here, your goal is to bridge the gap between friend/follower/fan and customer. When you have permission to send marketing materials to a customer, you can send targeted messages, whether through an auto-responder series, with ads in the e-newsletter, or with solo email marketing messages. In any case, it's a more effective and expedited way to get people into your sales funnel for monetization.

THE LIST: LEVERAGING YOUR SOCIAL MEDIA TRIPLE F'S (FRIENDS, FOLLOWERS, AND FANS)

I've heard many gurus, marketers, and publishers brag about their followers. They'll say things such as, "I have more than a thousand fans on Facebook" or "I have more than 2,000 followers on Twitter." Then I'll ask them how many free e-zine subscribers they have and ask about their list size. And they'll reply, "I haven't had time to build a list yet. I don't have an e-newsletter."

Well, in my opinion, they've won only half the battle....

It's fantastic that they have a following—people who seem to be interested in their messages (posts) and who have even perhaps bought into their overall philosophy. They can certainly cultivate these relationships to assist in their marketing efforts. However, I tell these gurus, "*They* (the fans) are following *you*! You don't own their email address. You don't have a list."

In the publishing world, a list (contact information of free or paid subscribers) is sacred. It's one of the most valuable things you own. You protect it and treat it with care, because your list is your financial bread and butter. It's made up of people—customers and subscribers—who can make or break your business through their purchasing power or lack thereof.

Your list is also your leverage—what you use when reaching out to other synergistic publishers and friendly competitors to swap marketing messages. In a reciprocal ad swap, you and another publisher agree to advertise to each other's lists. You run an ad in your publication for that publisher and they "reciprocate" and run an ad for you in their publication. There is no sharing or renting of the actual email addresses. Each publisher just runs the other publisher's advertisement. The list size is generally the same on both sides, and so is the message format that's agreed on: either a solo email or an e-newsletter sponsorship ad.

So, if you're an online publisher, guru, or business owner that has social media followers but no list, you're at a disadvantage. Initiate a plan to capture their email addresses and get permission to open up the personal lines of communication.

Twitter Caveat

My biggest concern with Twitter is sending out the right tweets and getting the right people to follow. By the "right people," I mean people who are targeted, relevant, and qualified individuals who are truly interested in your content. This is important because Twitter isn't like Facebook, where a user can accept or reject friend invitations. For the most part, with Twitter, people can just follow someone without being accepted by the tweeter.

 Note

I have seen some Twitter account owners protect their posts from public display via Tweet Privacy. This instills a certain level of privacy and follower qualification, but it isn't recommended if you're using Twitter for marketing purposes.

If you're using Twitter for your business, don't get wrapped up in building the number of followers you have or keeping track of how many retweets you get. Your ideal follower needs to bond with you on a deeper level. I believe that, with Twitter followers (or any social media followers for that matter!), quality is more important than quantity. The great Twitter challenge is to reach a level of bonding with your followers that's enough to get them to visit your website and convert (sign up to receive marketing communications or buy a product). Remember that many Twitter users follow someone arbitrarily and are just looking for return follows to help build their following list, for their own self-promotional or egotistical reasons. These people have a certain number in mind that they want to reach and focus on reaching that number no matter who they follow. In many instances, most Twitter users have nearly the same number of followers as the number of people they're following. Just because someone has a large number of followers doesn't mean he or she is actually resonating with them. Simply building one's number of followers is a shallow level of social networking interaction. There's no relevance to the follower—just reciprocation.

> Just because someone has a large number of followers doesn't mean he or she is actually resonating with them.

CONVERTING SOCIAL MEDIA FRIENDS, FOLLOWERS, AND FANS

I recommend that you make a special conversion effort to encourage social media followers to give share their email addresses with you—or, as we say, opt in to receive your marketing messages.

This typically involves creating strong promotional copy, which is sliced and diced and then used for social media posts and updates. This promotional copy drives followers to a lead-generation landing page (or squeeze page), where the goal is to capture the email address of the friend, follower, or fan.

The offer should be something that will resonate with your follower, such as a useful freebie—perhaps a bonus report, e-zine subscription, audio download, bonus video, webinar, or teleseminar. Ideally, this is something that has a perceived value and is immediate and relevant.

You run the campaign for a two-week period at a time, mixing your conversion messages with your regular, organic daily tweets or Facebook status updates. Then you monitor email sign-ups and website traffic (via Google Analytics), to ensure list growth and traffic source referrals.

Aside from captivating copy, many variables come into play to make sure the effort is successful. These include making sure email collection boxes are at the top, middle, and bottom of the lead-generation landing page being used. There should also be links to your privacy policy and an assurance statement alleviating any concern about email addresses being rented or sold to third parties.

It's also critical to clearly disclose *before* users submit their email address that opting in to receive your freebie also gives them a complementary subscription to your e-newsletter (if applicable), along with special messages and offers from time-to-time.

Finally, you should follow up with a series of autoresponder (targeted messages) emails welcoming the new subscriber, offering strong editorial content and special offers. These emails facilitate bonding; validates that the correct email was given; ensures that the user is aware of the sign-up; and helps reduce false "do not mail" reports, email bounces, and general attrition.

5

What Is Content?

When most people think of content, they think of contextual work—articles, books, newsletters, loose-leaf binders, magazines, trade papers, and so on. In essence, they think of work that is editorial in nature and delivered via the Web, email, or print.

My definition of content is broader and includes nearly any useful information that your end user will find relevant and beneficial, including audio, video, PowerPoint slides, or other presentation material.

When you start using your content to drive business efforts, you have to think beyond the normal use of content—that is, expand your view on the different types of content and how you can use it outside of its original format.

To get the most out of your content, you need to be a creative and strategic thinker. It's all about recycling, repurposing, repackaging, refreshing, rebundling, and republishing—all effective ways to leverage your content.

Content also can be used for bonding, lead generation, and sales. For example, you could

- Repackage, reformat, and send a group of old articles as a bonus report to your subscribers. This is a great tool for bonding or to use as a good-will gift.

- You could also take an old interview transcript and repurpose it into a press release or white paper that is offered as incentive in exchange for a prospect's email address. This is a great tactic for lead generation.

- Finally, you could take a bunch of related audios, have them transcribed, and offer them as paid e-books. This is a great way to create a front-end product line (products at a price point below $99 each).

Reusing and revamping content is also a key component in product development. For example, let's say you have several standalone paid e-books each on a different topic. You can go through your products and look for synergies between some of the e-books—ways to tie them together—make minor edits as necessary so each book dovetails each other; create a "blueprint" e-book that explains what's in each book and how to get the most out of them; then offer the new bundled product at a higher price point than the individual e-books alone.

But before you embark on recycling your content, you have to be aware of all the possible places content may be found. As mentioned in Chapter 1, "Content Rules!," you can get content from a variety of common sources, including these:

- Webinars

- Interviews (transcripts)

- Conference calls

- Event audio or video

- Old products

- Bonus reports

- Press releases

- Presentations (PowerPoint slides)

- Research papers

- Articles

Making the Most of Your Video Content

Video content is a great way to expand your market visibility as well as drive traffic to your website. Often, publishers think first and foremost about contextual content and overlook the value proposition of video.

Although video content has become popular in the last several years, many marketers upload video to YouTube, but they really don't know how to exactly leverage this platform for optimal online marketing results.

 Note

> First, let's reiterate that video is content, and content should be leveraged and syndicated. This helps with back-links, SEO, website visibility, branding, traffic generation, and buzz.

The best video-sharing sites to upload your videos to are YouTube, Google Video, MetaCafe, Blip.tv, and DailyMotion. These sites are extremely popular and get the most traffic and visitors.

Don't forget that you can also syndicate your video content through Really Simple Syndication (RSS), if you have it on your website. Following are some quick tips for optimizing video for killer search engine and SONAR marketing results:

 Note

> You may need to consult with your webmaster or website programmer regarding tagging your videos accordingly or inserting certain codes for usability.

1. Keep clips less than 5 minutes in length (1–3 minutes), and make sure they're relevant, beneficial, and interesting to users. Your video clips also could be teasers (excerpts or snippets) that link to a fuller-length video on your website.

2. Give your video a powerful, eye-catching title. This is where good copywriting skills come into play. Try to think of a great headline that would stop you dead in your tracks. This is the most important element of the video, because you only have a few seconds to grab your prospect's attention and make him or her click to watch.

3. Pack your title and description full of your top keywords—keywords that are in your video and that your target audience will search for.

4. Make sure your video is tagged (metadata) properly with your keywords to get picked up by search engine spiders.

5. Make sure your video includes either your company logo or your URL, for branding.

6. Cross-market your video in your e-newsletters, on your website, and in your social media accounts (Twitter, LinkedIn, and so on), to drive traffic and create buzz.

✉ *Note*

Best of all, depending on the video's creative approach, the viral factor could be off the charts, driving massive traffic to your website that can be parlayed into lead generation or cross-selling efforts.

7. If the video is on your website, encourage other users to republish it by offering the proper code that makes it easy for them to copy and paste. This helps with viral marketing.

When done right, marketing with video content can be a cost-effective, efficient, and powerful way to get prospects and profits.

...marketing with video content can be a cost-effective, efficient, and powerful way to get prospects and profits.

Content for Product Development

As mentioned earlier in the book, your content is critical to your sales funnel, moving the end user from prospect to subscriber and then to customer.

If you have an online business or are thinking about launching one, it's important to attract your prospects with a "free" product. Your customer content funnel (as described in Chapter 1) then consists of a few front-end products and, if possible, at least one midpoint and one back-end product.

Consider this sample of different info-based product-pricing levels:

- Free newsletter, report, teleseminar, and webinar

- Paid reports, paid newsletter, and continuity programs

- Bundled products, kits, and membership sites

- Conferences and events

- Premium services, upscale events, and other big-ticket items

- Lifetime value clubs and VIP products

Figure 5.1 shows an example of how you might set products at various levels.

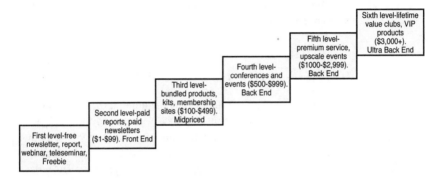

Figure 5.1   *An example of your product development levels or product pricing steps.*

 Note

Remember, the pricing steps shown in Figure 5.1 might not work with your business model. For instance, your company might sell a service or retail items instead of contextual-based info-products. However, this example gives you an idea about pricing structure and product variety.

To get the most out of your products, I recommend that you go through your entire product line at least twice a year to see if you can bundle products to create an entirely new product and price point.

For instance, if your company publishes e-books that are all front-end products, you might find a common thread among your e-books that you can use to develop a bundled kit. You can update and edit your e-books accordingly and add some new component pieces, such as a welcome letter, an interactive workbook, and a "blueprint" piece (explaining the objective of the kit, what you should get out of it, and how the e-books in the kit work together). You might decide to turn a related audio file into a CD. In addition, if you find similar material that is informational but perhaps not as explicit, you could create bonus e-books. You see, you've just repurposed content to create an entirely new product at a higher price point. The rest of the project now falls to graphics production and marketing.

Bundled products are a great midpoint or back-end product. The components, information, complexity, and other variables determine your final retail price point determined.

Consider these tips for creating new content-based products:

- Look through your content to see if the information is still valuable and fresh. You might need to freshen dates or references to specific reference points (in time). But good content is good content and is typically evergreen, meaning that it has a very long life. There's no need for it to collect dust. Repurpose, repackage, and reprice it!

STAYING ON THE UP AND UP

Keep in mind that it's a best practice to let the consumer know that some or all of the repurposed content has been recycled. You can do this in a few ways, including in the new product's promotional copy (either in the body text or as a disclaimer) or in the product's text, such as the introduction copy, a footnote or source, or disclaimer. For example, let's say you have DVD of a live event, which I'll call "New York, 2010," and you're now taking the DVD content and repurposing it into a new DVD, but adding extra features such as a resources page within the DVD, preferred links, and a glossary. You may want to say in the promotional copy that this new product contains footage from the original "New York 2010"event as well as bonus extras (then name all the new, value-added bonus features). This is a good way to support full disclosure of the old product but also touts the benefits of the new, recycled product.

- Consider making a transcript from a conference call or video event either a free report for your list (for bonding efforts), a lead-generation tool (for email collection), or a low-cost paid report to help new subscribers get to know you. This is a great way to fully utilize all your content opportunities.

- Take like-minded or themed content from several newsletter issues and create a "best of" report. Even better, you can offer this as a special holiday bonus or an introductory bonus to your new subscribers so that they can see the best of your best content in action.

If you decide to reuse some of your content for lead generation or other purposes, consider some additional points:

- **Macro, not micro**—For free reports, keep your content valuable but more general in nature. You'll want to save the nitty-gritty details—the how-tos and the specific actionable advice—for your paid version of the report. A great example comes from financial publishing. Your free report will have information about general market conditions or trends and may touch upon niche areas. But the deeper information, such as specific recommendations on certain stocks, indexes, or sectors, should be reserved for the paid version.

- **Quality and quantity**—Typically, free bonus reports, the ones that are really well-received by readers, are between 5 and 15 pages. You don't want a report to be too short, because the reader may feel gypped despite the fact that the content was free. The reader has an internal expectation, especially because she submitted her email address to receive this information. Keep the report length modest and the information relevant and useful.

- **Market surveillance and product viability**—Free reports are a fantastic way to gauge market interest or sentiment—especially before jumping in with both feet to launch a similar new product under the same subject matter. Before you spend time, money, and resources on something your customers or the marketplace might not find appealing, put your toe in the water first. For instance, let's say you're thinking about offering a copywriting coaching service to your customers. Start out by measuring internal sentiment. Create a simplified version of this product that contains the essence of your intended service, such as a short e-book called *50 Hot Copywriting Tips*. Price it attractively and promote it to your list. If the members on your list respond well to the e-book, they'll likely respond well to a more comprehensive version of the e-book, whether it involves multimedia components (such as a workbook, DVD, or CD) or a personal coaching element.

USE A PPC CAMPAIGN TO TEST MARKET VIABILITY

You can get an idea of general market interest by starting a two-week campaign on pay-per-click. Create several relevant, powerful ads, each with a different angle. Have each ad redirect to the same relevant landing page. Also make sure your landing page copy is strong and related to the ads. Pick strategic keywords and set an adequate budget for good ad exposure. After a few weeks, look at your click-through and conversion rates. If your landing page receives little or no click-throughs, you can conclude that the subject matter isn't resonating with the general marketplace.

Content for Syndication

When choosing content that you're using for syndication—regardless of whether it's done automatically, such as with RSS feeds, or manually with article marketing—make sure you use your best articles that will truly hit home with your target prospect.

These articles should have strong, attention-grabbing headlines; cover newsworthy subjects; and tap into emotional drivers. You need your headline to be strong because you have only about three seconds to capture someone's attention. Yours isn't the only editorial content out there vying for the attention of your target prospects; they're also receiving other RSS feeds and have bookmarked several article marketing sites. You need a headline that packs a punch and a follow-up story that truly delivers.

I've worked for several major newsletter publishers, and I've done some research and testing over the years to determine what kinds of headlines really work. Here's what I've found:

- Use headlines that tap into key emotional drivers, such as greed, fear, or vanity.

- Ask a relevant question, provoking a reader to read more.

- Be specific (use a specific dollar amount, percentage, reference in time, or other metric).

- Incorporate notable names from your industry to grab the readers' attention.

- Incorporate a current event that somehow affects your reader directly.

- Use a powerful call to action.

- Feature forecasts or trends (this is specifically good in health or financial industries and is more powerful at the beginning and end of the year).

- Mention or reveal something secret, unknown, rare, or breakthrough. People like to feel that they're reading something no one else has seen yet.

- Use "top xx" lists, such as "Top 5 Ways to Stand Out in the Mail" or "Top 3 Ways to Get the Promotion You've Always Wanted."

Over the years, I've also noted what didn't work with readers. Here are some of the top losers:

- Don't sound too high level. You want to sound educated, but not clinical or academic.

- Don't sound too cold. Your headline should speak *to*, not *at*, the reader. It must strike an emotional nerve.

- Avoid being too cheesy. Online readers have become more sophisticated and typically don't like headlines that are corny or cliché.

Seven Emotional Drivers

Most people can relate and respond to seven emotional drivers, regardless of their age or sex. These drivers strike an emotional nerve with the reader and prompt them to take action—whether it's to click, open, read, or buy. They're powerful, and they work. If you want to give your content life, tapping into one of these hot buttons is essential:[1]

Fear

Anger

Greed

Guilt

Exclusivity

Salvation

Vanity

> If you want to give your content life, tapping into one of these hot buttons is essential...

Similarly, most people strive for 10 general goals in life. They like reading articles to help them on their journey. Those standard wants are listed here:[2]

- To be healthier (including physical appearance)

- To be wealthier

- To be wiser

- To be more self-confident

- To be more secure

- To save time or money

- To advance professionally

- To find a work/home life balance

---

1. Anthony Chambers, Sales HQ—http://saleshq.monster.com/training/articles/635—7-emotional-sales-triggers-that-make-people-buy.

2. Joe Greenfield, http://ezinearticles.com/?Use-One-of-These-7-Great-Motivators-to-Ensure-Online-Marketing-Success!&id=4495606.

- To receive praise from others
- To not be alone

If you learn to weave these emotional triggers and related words through relevant editorial content and a powerful headline, you position your content for readership, which can lead to increased goal conversion.

Know Your List!

The most important rule in publishing is to know your list, your audience, or your subscribers. Knowing your current readers also helps you find new, targeted prospects.

If you haven't done so, I strongly recommend that you conduct at least one subscriber survey per year (most of my clients conduct two per year—one at the midpoint and one at the end of the year).

This survey should include demographic, geographic, and physiographic questions (see Figure 5.2). Find out who your subscribers are, what other newsletters they're reading, what their interests are, and things they like and dislike.

The more you know about your audience, the easier it will be for you to write useful and relevant information. Knowing who makes up your list and gearing specific content for your audience will get your articles read and passed around to like-minded readers.

You can use the data in your survey to create a *subscriber profile* to help familiarize both editorial and marketing staff with critical information about who an ideal subscriber is. If you understand your ideal subscriber, you'll understand your target prospect. This information is invaluable for acquisition and retention efforts, so make it readily available to key staff members for easy reference. It's a constant reminder of who you're writing for and who you'd like to add to your database. In addition to its editorial and marketing uses, this information can help with media buying, joint venture opportunities, and creative and product development.

Demographic
- Age: 25-65 years old
- Sex:
    - 20% Male
    - 80% Female
- College:
    - 80% yes
- Own home
    - 90% yes
- Individual Income:
    - $75,000-$200,000/year
- Work habits:
    - Mostly retirees: no
    - Mostly professionals: yes

Psychographic:
- Interests:
    - Achieve professional success; make money; continue higher education
- Non-interests:
    - Working from home
- Reading habits or preferences:
    - Variety of articles in each issue focusing on different topics
    - Articles between 250 and 500 words
    - Newsletter frequency of 1X per week
    - Most subscribers read 75-100% of issue within 1-3 days of receiving it
- Purchasing habits:
    - 20% current buyers
    - 80% indicated interest and will purchase product in future
- Preferred information delivery preference:
    - Web-based (e-books, ezines)
    - Print
- Non-preferred information delivery preference:
    - Podcasts/MP3

Geographic:
- Top States:
    - NY (mostly democratic state based on 2004 election map)
    - FL
    - NJ
    - CA
    - TX
- Top Countries:
    - US
    - UK
    - Canada
    - Australia
    - New Zealand

Figure 5.2   *A sample subscriber profile. This helps familiarize a publisher with their customer and prospects.*

6

Learning and Leveraging the SONAR Content Distribution Model™

As I mentioned in the introduction to this book, I've been in marketing for nearly 20 years and have worked for top publishers for about half that time. I accomplished many objectives for these organizations, including building lists (increasing free newsletter subscribers), growing sales, and increasing website traffic. I also worked to expand website visibility and awareness.

Despite the fact that I led the marketing efforts for some of the most well-known publishers in the industry, I didn't necessarily have unlimited resources at my disposal. I typically had limited marketing budgets, and the members of my team usually consisted of either junior marketers who were right out of college or experienced marketers who were newbies to online marketing. This meant I had to be strategic and creative with my tactics and be able to articulate my plans effectively and easily for my marketing coordinators to implement.

For me, it's always easier to think of things in terms of processes. I try to evaluate a situation and identify a process or system that enhances the objective and streamlines the tactical efforts involved to get the expected results. It's similar to creating a mathematical formula.

However, this "formula" also needs to be cost-effective and measurable. As a direct marketer, I need to be able to measure my efforts to validate the time and resources (even limited resources) spent on achieving results. This can all be tied to the return on investment (ROI) for each campaign, to show whether the effort breaks even. Although I didn't always have the marketing budget available to implement large advertising campaigns, I did have a lot of something else—content. So, I sat down one night at my home computer and started to look at my content resources and my goals. I then looked at all the free online platforms that I could use to leverage the content and achieve those goals.

But I needed a catchy name—something easy to remember for my team of junior marketers, and something that would simplify the process and stick in their minds, similar to the "hook" of a good pop song.

Many years ago, when I was just out of college and going on interviews in New York City, I often used acronyms to help me remember responses for those typical canned questions that human resources personnel asked, such as, "What are some of your best characteristics?" or "What will help me remember you out of everyone else being interviewed for this job?"

Being inexperienced and not having much leverage to bring to the table, I had to play up my innate characteristics to illustrate my capabilities, integrity, and work ethic. One of the tricks I used to help me remember this information was the acronym FROME, which stood for friendly, reliable, organized, motivated, and energetic. It might seem juvenile, but it worked. Remembering FROME helped me answer quickly with confidence and conviction—no matter how nervous I was. And I always nailed the interview.

Think about it. MASH. SCUBA. FBI. CIA—these are terms that are easier to remember with the use of an acronym.

So, I thought of a memorable acronym to illustrate my new systematic process for leveraging content on the Web: the SONAR Content Distribution Model™.

What Is SONAR Marketing?

I first wrote about SONAR on my blog, MuscleMarketing.Blogspot.com, in June 2007 and then later in the Early to Rise (ETR) daily e-zine. ETR is part of publishing powerhouse Agora, Inc. For more than two years, I led the online marketing efforts at ETR and headed the graphics, customer service, fulfillment, and web marketing departments as the vice president of marketing and business development. I was also in charge of passing on new and innovative marketing, PR, and media buying strategies to the staff, and I spearheaded product development.

SONAR is a cost-effective yet powerful method of repurposing and synchronizing content (text, audio, or video) distribution into various, targeted channels. It is a systematic approach that enables companies, publishers, entrepreneurs—anyone with content—to turn traffic into sales or lead generation.

For example, if you have an article in your e-newsletter or recent blog post on or around the same time the same article or post is being published in your e-letter, repurpose it and distribute it using the SONAR Content Distribution Model™.

SONAR represents the following online distribution platforms:

S: Syndicate partners, content syndication networks, and user-generated content sites

O: Online press releases

N: Network (social) communities and social bookmarking sites

A: Article directories

R: Relevant posts to blogs, forums, and message boards

In my experience, implementing these techniques into your online marketing mix and optimizing your website to harness the traffic it will bring (capturing leads and sales) will have a dramatic impact on your web traffic and prospecting efforts.

The following sections break down the SONAR acronym and illustrates the various online distribution platforms (channels) the content stems from and gets repurposed to—similar to the spokes that extend from the center of a wheel—the SONAR content distribution wheel.

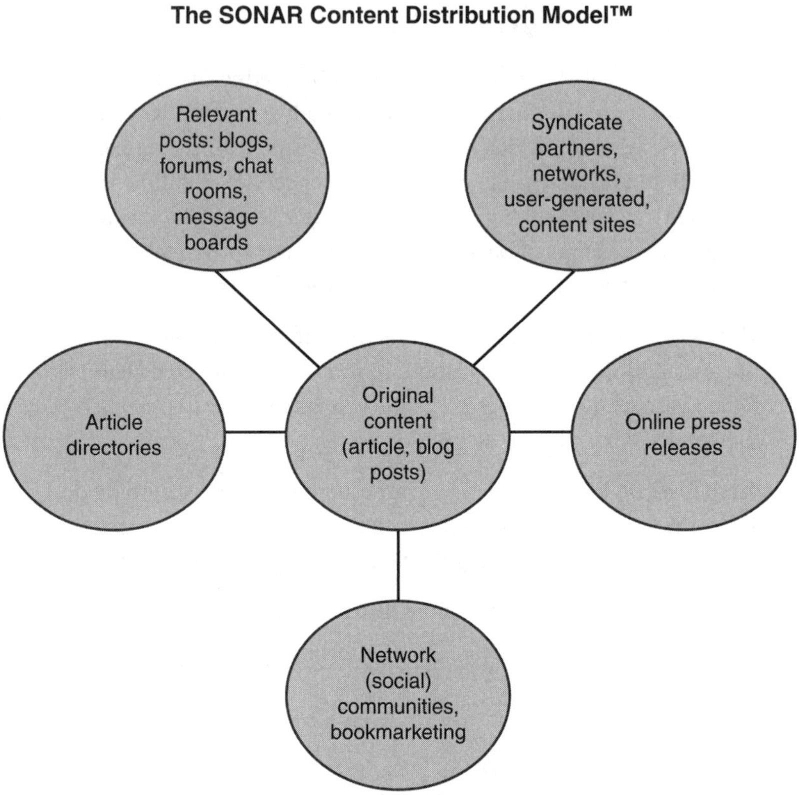

The SONAR Content Distribution Model™

Figure 6.1   *SONAR content distribution wheel*

S: Syndicate Partners, Content Syndication Networks, and User-Generated Content Sites

The *S* in *SONAR* stands for syndicate partners, content syndication networks, and user-generated content sites. Each of these is explained in the following sections.

Syndicate Partners

Syndicate partners are those synergistic contacts that you've either cultivated or need to build to help spread your articles around the Web. They're random websites and publishers that are looking for useful, relevant content about your subject matter so that they can republish it either on their website or in their newsletter. These are also called editorial contributions or guest editorials. Because the foundation of the syndicate partners list pertains to the relevance for your individual business, this list may be different for each business. In other words, no two lists may be alike. Your syndicate partners are custom to your businesses content, needs, and objectives.

Note

Just to clarify, syndicate partners are not licensing your content (paying a fee to use your content). That is a different business model entirely. Syndicate partners are simply websites, newsletters, and publishers you coordinate with to share editorial content in exchange for non-monetary compensation, such as an author byline or editorial note with short description of your publication and back-link to your website.

Finding sites to partner with on an editorial basis means networking at industry events, conducting market research, and even "cold emailing" or "cold calling" sites to explain the mutually beneficial value of an editorial exchange.

For example, let's say you have a financial newsletter with great content and credentialed writers, and you want to extend its reach. When searching the Web, you can use search terms such as "financial article submission sites," "submit article, financial," or "submit article, investing." The latter search pulls in the meta description in the search results for sites that have a platform for article submission, such as these sites:

- www.themarketfinancial.com/submit-articles

- www.financialsense.com/about-us/contributors/process

- http://seekingalpha.com/page/submit-an-article

- www.investingvalue.com/submit-investing-article.htm

When looking for a publishing partner, you need to evaluate that publisher's reach (website traffic, Alexa traffic rank, and list size) and synergy to your own site. You must have commonality in the subject matter you're both publishing and a like-mindedness readership. However, you can also complement each other's editorial content and fill in voids that you are not currently writing about.

Content Syndication Networks

Content syndication networks are much easier to define. These are reputable sites that coordinate the distribution of publishers' content. Some networks are fee based, but others rely on income from the advertisers within their network. This is a great way to encourage your content to go viral and pierce social networking and article sites. Examples of content syndication networks include the following:

- http://synnd.com/

- www.mochila.com/

User-Generated Content Sites

User-generated content sites, or "Web 2.0" sites, are websites that enable users to add, edit, and upload their own content (audio, video, or contextual). These Web 2.0 sites have overlap with some more recognizable social media sites in use today. A moderator typically reviews content before publishing it.

According to the eBiz MBA Knowledgebase, some of the most popular user-generated websites include these:

- YouTube
- Wikipedia
- Craigslist
- Twitter
- WordPress
- IMBD
- Flickr
- PhotoBucket
- eHow
- Digg
- TypePad
- HubPages
- DeviantArt
- Wikia

O: Online Press Releases

The *O* in *SONAR* stands for online press releases.

Distributing press releases and public relations efforts has long been an effective way to push out targeted messages and influence public opinion. Only with the birth of the Internet have marketers started to leverage the immediacy and cost-effectiveness of both free and paid online distribution platforms.

However, SONAR marketing takes leveraging online press releases one step further. Sure, you can use SONAR tactics to disseminate legitimate, newsworthy messages, such as a company milestone, a product launch, a change in leadership, an award or accolade, and other business news. But if you are also a publisher—meaning that you publish articles, newsletters, or blog posts—then you can also harness the power of your content using press releases.

First, you need to understand how a standard press release is formatted—the basic layout, the type of information that must be included, and the third-person voice.

Second, you need to know how to write and repurpose articles that are friendly to both search engines and human readers. Writing for the Web is slightly different than writing for traditional media outlets. Keep in mind that you're not reinventing the wheel and creating new content. You're simply repurposing your strongest articles to read as press releases. You might need to add some transitional sentences for flow, but ultimately, you're working with already published content and tweaking it for its new use.

For example, any newsletter articles that you've written or blog posts that meet the following criteria are ideal for online press release distribution:

> # Writing for the Web is slightly different than writing for traditional media outlets.

- A breakthrough

- A milestone

- Recent survey results or data

- Controversial or contrarian viewpoint

- Lists or steps to do something—how-tos

Finally, you need to know where to disseminate your online press release. I use several free online services, such as Free-press-release.com and Prlog.org. Some platforms have limited word counts, so you might need to tighten up long headlines or edit body copy as you copy and paste your release to different PR websites.

If you want added exposure, I suggest that you occasionally use a paid online PR service for the really important news that will complement your weekly SONAR efforts.

 Note

I use PRWeb because it has a variety of rate packages, depending on how much coverage you want, and it offers decent analytic reporting that illustrates full-page reads, headline impressions, search engine hits, and geographic pickup.

Press releases are effective vehicles for creating buzz and assisting in your search engine optimization (SEO) efforts through back-links—that is, links from other blogs and websites that have picked up your release and republished it on their websites.

Your ultimate goal is for media, bloggers, and online news aggregators, such as Google News and Yahoo! News, to snatch up your online release and republish it.

PRESS FOR PENNIES: FIVE EASY WAYS TO LEVERAGE ONLINE PRESS RELEASES

1. Although most free PR distribution services have a release template (and a keyword selection tool) that you can use to upload your release, consider using a standard PR template as a guide. This helps ensure that your release is constructed as a legitimate press release. I often use this website: www.press-release-writing.com/press-release-template.htm.

2. It's important to make sure your press release is newsworthy, is well written, and has value-oriented information. It shouldn't be self-serving (that is, blatantly promoting yourself or your website). It should be editorial in nature and have a strong, keyword-rich headline, subhead, and lead (introductory paragraph). Because search engine spiders scan pages from top to bottom, your top 10 keywords should also be heaviest (densest) from the top of the document to the bottom. Some helpful keyword search tools include http://freekeywords.wordtracker.com/ and https://adwords.google.com/select/KeywordToolExternal. These tools help you identify keywords that have good search volume and fit your target audience.

3. Another basic (but often overlooked) PR tactic is to make sure your release is written in the third person and that you include one to three quotes about the main person the release is built around. Don't forget to use spell check and proof your release. If the release contains spelling or grammatical errors, it will ruin your credibility. Remember to include only one or two links to your website at the bottom of the release, such as "To read the full article or schedule interviews, contact [add your web address]."

4. Recycle your e-newsletter content through press releases. Repurpose editorial content to be exciting, newsworthy, and consumer driven. You can often use the same copy, with minor edits for flow and format.

> 5. If you use a PR distribution service, such as PRWeb or Business Wire (for a nominal fee), that syndicates your story to traditional media outlets and national publications, complement that effort by reaching out to local and regional newspapers via their websites. In addition, use top, free, online press services such as www.PRlog.org, www.free-press-release.com, and www.i-newswire.com.
>
> *Source:* http://musclemarketing.blogspot.com/2007/06/leveraging-online-press-releasescompany.html

N: Network (Social) Communities and Social Bookmarking Sites

The *N* in *SONAR* stands for network (social) communities and bookmarking sites, which are explained in this section.

Another SONAR tactic is to return to repurposed content and upload relevant and useful "nuggets" in related social communities and bookmarking sites.

 Note

Remember to keep these nuggets short and focused. Many of these sites—such as Twitter—have character-count limits, possibly as few as 140 characters.

Hundreds, probably thousands, of social communities and bookmarking sites exist. Some are general and others are niche.

Social networks enable users to join groups of like-minded individuals and correspond with each other via posts. You can add friends and participate in discussions. The networks enable interaction and exchange of information.

Social bookmarking occurs when members can save (or "bookmark"), organize, and search websites that they find interesting. Other members in the network with like-minded interests can then view these sites to read more. This is a great way for content to go viral and get passed around, generating buzz and traffic to the related website or article.

The site you choose to market on helps shape your marketing message. For example, if you're using Twitter, your messages are limited to only 140 characters. Facebook allows more text—around 1,000 characters—so your message can be quite different (although still short). Regardless of which site you choose, your messages need to be short and powerful. Most important, they need to link somewhere—your main article page, your newsletter archives, your sign-up page, or some URL that is part of your main website.

According to the eBiz MBA Knowledgebase, these are among the most popular social networking sites:

> Regardless of which site you choose, your messages need to be short and powerful.

- Facebook
- MySpace
- Twitter
- LinkedIn (professional networking)
- Ning
- Tagged
- Classmates
- Hi5
- MyYearbook
- MeetUp

The eBiz MBA Knowledgebase also provides this list of popular social bookmarking sites:

- Twitter
- Digg
- YahooBuzz
- Reddit
- StumbleUpon
- Delicious
- Tweetmeme
- Mixx
- FARK
- SlashDot

LEVERAGING LINKEDIN: THE PROFESSIONAL SOCIAL NETWORK

If you haven't established a presence on LinkedIn, I strongly recommend that you create a profile and link away.

LinkedIn is one of the top five social networks on the Web and focuses on linking professionals through networking opportunities, business discussions, information exchanges, Q&As, industry news, professional groups, and more.

It's easy and free to get started. Go to LinkedIn.com and create your profile. You can add information about your education and career. And through your account settings, you can choose what information you want to keep private and what you'd like to display for others in your network to view.

It's also helpful to get and give recommendations because it validates your credentials as an expert in your field. After you sign up, you can invite colleagues and business partners to join your network, and you can join various groups that relate to your industry. After you join those groups, you'll receive weekly messages from the group leader regarding group discussions and other useful information. You will also be able to view other group members' profiles and invite those you think could be synergistic to your business to join your network.

Joining LinkedIn can help your business and your website in several ways:

- **SEO**—You can write and upload useful articles and start discussions regarding information that benefits your fellow members. Articles should be relevant and contain value-oriented information. When you upload an excerpt from an article or piece of news, you can enter a link to the source, which ideally should be the original content housed on your website (in your newsletter archives). This educates your fellow group members and encourages traffic to your site to read the full article. If your site is optimized with tools to monetize traffic, you can leverage the traffic for leads and possibly sales. You can easily identify the traffic with Google website analytics by looking for LinkedIn as a referring source page.

- **Advertising**—You can easily alert members of your special skills, expertise, or services. LinkedIn now has special segmented areas within each group for "promotional" messages. Pay attention to each group's rules for posting these types of messages, and abide by the rules. Abuse within the group or continued posting of irrelevant, useless, or "spam" messages could lead to expulsion from the group and perhaps even get you banned from LinkedIn. However, if done correctly and within the guidelines of LinkedIn, you have an opportunity to network with responders, share ideas, and cultivate business relationships. The key is to be relevant. In addition, members can post a classified-type ad in the job section.

- **Increased web presence**—If your goal is to improve your website's presence, being actively involved in LinkedIn is critical. If you spend a little time each day or reserve one day a week for group participation (by providing expert answers to relevant Q&As, engaging in targeted discussions, or uploading useful information), your name and brand will be prominent within the site. This not only establishes you as an expert within LinkedIn, but it also can drive ancillary traffic to your website from members and referrals looking for more great information. And the more traffic your site gets, the more it helps your organic search ranking and visibility.

Source: http://musclemarketing.blogspot.com/2009/05/leveraging-linked-in.html

A: Article Directories

The *A* in *SONAR* stands for article directories, which this section explains.

Leveraging content in top article directories is the foundation of article marketing. As mentioned earlier in this book, the utility of the article and the relevance to the target reader is most important. When you have your original content, you can slice and dice it into smaller versions to upload on various article directories.

As with most of the content being leveraged for the Web, articles that are useful, pertinent, keyword rich, and easy to read generate the best results. Within the article body (if allowed by site) or in the author field, you should include a link to the full article or your newsletter archive. This is the call to action that helps drive traffic to your website.

As with the other online platforms, you can find both general and niche article directories. You can find specialized ones with a simple Internet search using keywords in your area of expertise (health, marketing, investing, business opportunity, and more).

Friday Traffic Report lists these popular article directory sites:

- Ezinearticles
- Helium
- ArticleDashboard

- ArticleBase

- GoArticles

- Buzzle

- AmericanChronicle

- ArticlesFactory

- Amazines

- SelfGrowth

R: Relevant Posts to Blogs, Forums, and Message Boards

Finally, the *R* in *SONAR* stands for relevant posts to blogs, forums, and message boards. Each is explained in this section.

Crafting messages for blogs, forums, chat rooms, and message boards takes experience and finesse. As you read in Chapter 4, "What Came First: The Guerrilla or the Web?," rules of engagement apply to this tactic. You need to create an organic presence within the forum and start engaging with other users. Do this for about a month before you start tactfully seeding the forum with your advertorial message. I say "advertorial" because your posts will be editorial in nature (useful, relevant, and beneficial) but

> Crafting messages for blogs, forums, chat rooms, and message boards takes experience and finesse.

also have an underlying marketing goal. Your messages shouldn't come across as blatant self-serving promotional plugs; they should have some sort of educational purpose for the other members and be relevant to each sub topic or category within the blog, forum, or message board. As I mentioned in Chapter 4, I mix up my advertorial messages instead of limiting them to just one website.

For example, let's say that my client is ABC website and that the company is in the health industry. Before I start my campaign for ABC, I get familiar with the forum and the various subsections to see what's best suited for my participation. After a month or so of contributing to discussions with no ulterior motive, I might mention some great article I read on the health industry. I mention my client, ABC, but I also mention other useful articles from other relevant publishers. This shows a sharing of knowledge and a general appreciation for relevant editorial information—not just a bias toward ABC website.

Because this SONAR distribution platform is very targeted, the forums, blogs, bulletin boards, and chat rooms you decide to frequent will be dynamic, always changing. Ultimately, what you pick depends on relevance—your message, niche, and target audience.

Some popular forums are general in nature but have specialized subsections. I frequent these forums under this category:

- Topix.com
- WarriorForum.com
- Forums.offtopic.com
- Amazon.com
- Politico.com
- Gaiaonline.com/forum
- Messages.yahoo.com/

If you're not sure which niche forums and message boards are right for you, check out BoardReader (http://boardreader.com/), where you can search for targeted forums using general terms such as *health*, *investing*, and *marketing*.

SONAR in Action: Putting It All Together

SONAR is a tactic I've been deploying for several years—for my own business, for the companies I've worked for, and for my consulting clients. And it's never failed.

To show a real-life example of how to reposition original content and distribute it to the various SONAR channels, I'm including an original article by a former client, AppleBoost, which published an alternative health e-newsletter called *Nutrition Intelligence Report* (NIR).

The article was written by Suzanne Dixon, MPH, MS, RD, an internationally recognized expert in nutrition, chronic disease, cancer, and health and wellness. This article is a classic example of great content that can be repurposed and leveraged in each of the five SONAR distribution channels (also known as the SONAR content wheel, shown in Figure 6.1).

Although the original article and its repurposed spin-offs currently appear all over the Web, AppleBoost's president, Dave Copeland, graciously granted me permission to use one of NIR's most popular articles to illustrate the SONAR Content Distribution Model™ in the real world.

It's important to show the original content source and its many repurposed uses for increased website visibility, SEO, and traffic generation.

Original Article Source

The following is the original content—the pure editorial use—as published in Nutrition Intelligence Report e-newsletter as well as in the newsletter archives. Note the length, the headline, the subheads, and other formatting, as these are elements that will be modified during the SONAR content wheel process.

SONAR Channel: Original content

Source: AppleBoost.com

January 26, 2010

Issue #8: How to Turn Off the Cancer Switch

How Nutrition Can Thwart Three Steps of Cancer Development

By Suzanne W. Dixon, MPH, MS, RD

In the world of medical fears, few things rank as high as cancer. For many people, a cancer diagnosis challenges their view of themselves as a "healthy person." Fortunately, many cancers are curable. You can survive cancer and be healthy.

Cancer Biology 101

A basic understanding of how cancer develops can help you take advantage of what nutrition has to offer. Food can and should be a part of your plan for reducing the risk of cancer, and the risk of getting cancer again if you've already had it.

There are three basic steps to cancer development. Obviously, the process is very complicated at the cellular level. But the three-step model explains the most important changes that lead to cancer. These three steps represent some of the best opportunities for preventing cancer from developing at all.

Don't Be Initiated into This Club

The first step in cancer development is called initiation. One of the most common causes of initiation is free radical damage. Free radicals, which also go by the name oxidants, cause cell damage. Have you ever really thought about antioxidants? What is an oxidant? And why are we anti, or against, oxidants?

Oxidants cause oxidation, which is damaging to DNA—the instructions that tell cells what to do when. To wrap your head around oxidation, think of rusting.

Rusting is oxidation in the environment. Metal rusts and no longer functions as it should. This same process happens in the body. We don't exactly rust, but we do experience the same type of oxidation damage in our bodies.

This is where nutrition comes in. Vegetables, fruit, whole grains, legumes, nuts, and seeds—plant foods—are loaded with antioxidants, and not just the common antioxidants we all know and love. Beyond vitamin C, vitamin E, and beta-carotene are hundreds, even thousands of antioxidants in plant foods.

It's these thousands of antioxidants that work together to prevent oxidation in our bodies. In this very direct way, antioxidants in food prevent initiation. This is one of the ways plant foods are believed to reduce cancer risk.

But even with this plant protection, a few cells in our bodies are likely to be damaged, or initiated. The key to preventing cancer development also lies with the next step, called promotion.

One Promotion You Don't Want

The second step of the cancer-development process, called promotion, doesn't happen to just any cell. It happens to cells that already are initiated. We know plant foods limit the number of initiated cells, but what happens to the few cells that slip through the cracks?

Ideally, if a cell becomes damaged, it goes through a programmed cell death. This prevents it from multiplying and creating more damaged cells. However, for cells that are initiated but don't die, promotion, or step 2, can occur.

In promotion, damaged cells ignore the chemical messages of the normal cells around them. The damaged cell might be getting ready to multiply and grow. The normal cells in the neighborhood send chemical messages to prevent this. These messages say, "Stop, wait, don't go there." Promotion allows damaged cells to tune out the "stop" messages.

Here's where plant foods come to the rescue again. Among the thousands of nutrients found in plants are many that can help damaged cells hear the messages. These nutrients can, quite literally, act as little messengers. They make damaged cells sit up and take notice.

Dark purple and red foods seem to be especially adept at improving cellular communication. Think blackberries, blueberries, dark red cherries, grape juice, and red wine. Soy foods, such as tofu and tempeh, often touted for their possible effects on regulating female hormones (such as estrogen), have some antipromotion tricks up their sleeves as well.

And promotion is reversible. It's one of the only parts of cancer development that can actually be turned back! Plant foods can help a "deaf" cell hear again. In a sense, this can help a damaged cell become closer to normal.

Stop This Progress If You Can

This brings us to progression, the third step in cancer development. In progression, damaged cells take the communication problem one step further. Now these cells not only ignore messages; they begin to create their own messages. They try to influence the cells around them. It's like negative peer pressure.

This is the damaged cells' attempt to get normal cells to cooperate so they can grow and spread beyond the original site of cancer. This step is a key to metastasis—when cancer cells spread to distant parts of the body. This is important because it's only after cancer cells have spread that treating cancer becomes so difficult.

You guessed it. Plant foods have a role to play in blocking progression, too. Just as the thousands of naturally occurring phytonutrients in plants help damaged cells hear, they also help block unhealthy messages from damaged cells.

Many plant nutrients can act as roadblocks of a sort. They make it harder for damaged cells to influence the cells around them to misbehave, too. Several nutrients have been studied for their effects on preventing or slowing progression.

Resveratrol, found in red wine and grape juice; lycopene, found in cooked tomatoes, watermelon, and pink grapefruit; and quercetin, found in apples, tea, and onions, all seem particularly well suited for minimizing cancer cells' ability to go through the progression phase of cancer development.

Putting Plants to Work for You

Knowing that plants contain nutrients that can slow down and impede the cancer process is pretty motivating. Every time you put a healthy plant food on your plate, you'll feel good knowing you're giving your body the tools to keep cancer at bay.

And it doesn't hurt that these same foods help prevent other diseases as well. For preventing heart disease, diabetes, stroke, high blood pressure, arthritis, you name it—plants in the diet are nothing but helpful.

Every chance you get, throw in a plant food. You'll be on your way to better health. Blueberries on your oatmeal? Check. Apple with lunch? Check. Nuts in your afternoon yogurt? Check. Carrots and hummus as a snack while fixing dinner? Check. A heaping pile of veggies with dinner? Check. Green leafies on your sandwich? Check.

The options are endless. The choice is up to you.

S: Syndicate Partners, Content Syndication Networks, and User-Generated Content Sites

The following example shows the original article and how it was used on a syndicate partner's website for republication. Because this was the first republication of the article, I left the headline and subheads unchanged (since they are so powerful) and the remainder of the article is also virtually unchanged. My modifications were moving around/separating some paragraphs toward the end of the article, not including medical footnotes and references (which were on the original content's webpage), and adding a call to action and back-link to publisher's website for more information.

SONAR Channel: Syndicate partner

Source: HealthierTalk.com

==============================

How to Turn Off the Cancer Switch

By Suzanne Dixon on 03/12/2010

In the world of medical fears, few things rank as high as cancer. For many people, a cancer diagnosis challenges their view of themselves as a "healthy person." Fortunately, many cancers are curable. You *can* survive cancer and be healthy.

Cancer Biology 101

A basic understanding of how cancer develops can help you take advantage of what nutrition has to offer. Food can and should be a part of your plan for reducing the risk of cancer, and the risk of getting cancer again if you've already had it.

There are three basic steps to cancer development. Obviously, the process is very complicated at the cellular level. But the three-step model explains the most important changes that lead to cancer. These three steps represent some of the best opportunities for preventing cancer from developing at all.

Don't Be Initiated into This Club

The first step in cancer development is called initiation. One of the most common causes of initiation is free radical damage. Free radicals, which also go by the name oxidants, cause cell damage. Have you ever *really* thought about antioxidants? What is an oxidant? And why are we anti, or against, oxidants?

Oxidants cause oxidation, which is damaging to DNA—the instructions that tell cells what to do when. To wrap your head around oxidation, think of rusting.

Rusting is oxidation in the environment. Metal rusts, and it no longer functions as it should. This same process happens in the body. We don't exactly rust, but we do experience the same type of oxidation damage in our bodies.

This is where nutrition comes in. Vegetables, fruit, whole grains, legumes, nuts, and seeds—plant foods—are loaded with antioxidants. And not just the common antioxidants we all know and love. Beyond vitamin C, vitamin E, and beta-carotene are hundreds, even thousands of antioxidants in plant foods.

It's these thousands of antioxidants that work together to prevent oxidation in our bodies. In this very direct way, antioxidants in food prevent initiation. This is one of the ways by which plant foods are believed to reduce cancer risk.

But even with this plant protection, a few cells in our bodies are likely to be damaged, or initiated. The key to preventing cancer development also lies with the next step, called promotion.

One Promotion You Don't Want

The second step of the cancer-development process, called promotion, doesn't happen to just any cell. It happens to cells that already are initiated. We know plant foods limit the number of initiated cells, but what happens to the few cells that slip through the cracks?

Ideally, if a cell becomes damaged, it goes through a programmed cell death. This prevents it from multiplying and creating more damaged cells. However, for cells that are initiated but don't die, promotion, or step 2, can occur.

In promotion, damaged cells ignore the chemical messages of the normal cells around them. The damaged cell might be getting ready to multiply and grow. The normal cells in the neighborhood send chemical messages to prevent this. These messages say, "Stop, wait, don't go there." Promotion allows damaged cells to tune out the "stop" messages.

Here's where plant foods come to the rescue again. Among the thousands of nutrients found in plants are many that can help damaged cells hear the messages. These nutrients can, quite literally, act as little messengers. They make damaged cells sit up and take notice.

Dark purple and red foods seem to be especially adept at improving cellular communication. Think blackberries, blueberries, dark red cherries, grape juice, and red wine. Soy foods, such as tofu and tempeh, often touted for their possible effects on regulating female hormones (such as estrogen), have some antipromotion tricks up their sleeves as well.

And promotion is reversible. It's one of the only parts of cancer development that can actually be turned back! Plant foods can help a "deaf" cell hear again. In a sense, this can help a damaged cell become closer to normal.

Stop This Progress If You Can

This brings us to "progression," the third step in cancer development. In progression, damaged cells take the communication problem one step further. Now these cells not only ignore messages; they begin to create their own messages. They try to influence the cells around them. It's like negative peer pressure.

This is the damaged cells' attempt to get normal cells to cooperate so they can grow and spread beyond the original site of cancer. This step is a key to metastasis—when cancer cells spread to distant parts of the body. This is important because it's only after cancer cells have spread that treating cancer becomes so difficult.

You guessed it. Plant foods have a role to play in blocking progression, too. Just as the thousands of naturally occurring phytonutrients in plants help damaged cells hear, they also help block unhealthy messages from damaged cells.

Many plant nutrients can act as roadblocks of a sort. They make it harder for damaged cells to influence the cells around them to misbehave, too. Several nutrients have been studied for their effects on preventing or slowing progression.

Resveratrol, found in red wine and grape juice; lycopene, found in cooked tomatoes, watermelon, and pink grapefruit; and quercetin, found in apples, tea, and onions, all seem particularly well suited for minimizing cancer cells' ability to go through the progression phase of cancer development.

Putting Plants to Work for You

Knowing that plants contain nutrients that can slow down and impede the cancer process is pretty motivating. Every time you put a healthy plant food on your plate, you'll feel good knowing you're giving your body the tools to keep cancer at bay.

And it doesn't hurt that these same foods help prevent other diseases as well. For preventing heart disease, diabetes, stroke, high blood pressure, arthritis, you name it—plants in the diet are nothing but helpful.

Every chance you get, throw in a plant food. You'll be on your way to better health.

Blueberries on your oatmeal? Check. Apple with lunch? Check. Nuts in your afternoon yogurt? Check. Carrots and hummus as a snack while fixing dinner? Check. A heaping pile of veggies with dinner? Check. Green leafies on your sandwich? Check.

The options are endless. The choice is up to you.

For references or more information go here: www.appleboost.com/newsletters/2010/01/26/how-to-turn-off-the-cancer-switch/.

This example shows the original article and its repurposed use in a user-generated content site. Some of the minor differences from the original article include headline modification (I combined original headline with subheading from fifth paragraph) and length (word count limitation). On many sites, you'll find restrictions to word counts. In this case, I took what I believed to be a good synopsis of the article (the fifth paragraph) and used it as the descriptive text for Digg. With this particular usage, the entire excerpt (headline, URL mention, and text) is clickable to full article.

SONAR Channel: User-Generated Content Site

Source: Digg.com

===============================

How to Turn Off the Cancer Switch: Putting Plants to Work for You

appleboost.com—Knowing that plants contain nutrients that can slow down and impede the cancer process is pretty motivating. Every time you put a healthy plant food on your plate, you'll feel good knowing you're giving your body the tools to keep cancer at bay. And it doesn't hurt that these same foods help prevent other diseases as well. For preventing heart....

O: Online Press Releases

This example shows the original article and its repurposed use as a press release. As you can see, the headline remained the same. Modifications include content repurposing so it now reads in third person as well as content rearrangement turning former newsletter paragraphs into quotes.

The important call to action and back-link were added, as well as a short bio about the publisher to encourage website traffic and e-newsletter sign-ups.

SONAR Channel: Online press release

Source: Free-press-release.com

================================

How to Turn Off the Cancer Switch

FOR IMMEDIATE RELEASE

(Free-Press-Release.com) February 1, 2010—*Churubusco, NY— February 01, 2010*—In the world of medical fears, few things rank as high as cancer. For many people, a cancer diagnosis challenges their view of themselves as a "healthy person." Fortunately, many cancers are curable. Individuals can survive cancer and be healthy.

According to Suzanne Dixon, MPH, MS, RD, internationally recognized expert in nutrition, chronic disease, cancer, and health and wellness, and the executive editor of *Nutrition Intelligence Report*, "A basic understanding of how cancer develops can help you take advantage of what nutrition has to offer. Food can and should be a part of your plan for reducing the risk of cancer, and the risk of getting cancer again if you've already had it."

She adds, "There are three basic steps to cancer development. Obviously, the process is very complicated at the cellular level. But the three-step model explains the most important changes that lead to cancer. These three steps represent some of the best opportunities for preventing cancer from developing at all."

The first step in cancer development is called initiation. One of the most common causes of initiation is free radical damage. Dixon adds, "This is where nutrition comes in. Vegetables, fruit, whole grains, legumes, nuts, and seeds—plant foods—are loaded with antioxidants. And not just the common antioxidants we all know and love. Beyond vitamin C, vitamin E, and beta-carotene are hundreds, even thousands of antioxidants in plant foods."

The second step of the cancer-development process, called promotion, doesn't happen to just any cell. It happens to cells that already are initiated.

The third step in cancer development is progression. In progression, damaged cells take the communication problem one step further. These cells not only ignore messages; they begin to create their own messages. They try to influence the cells around them. It's like negative peer pressure.

Says Dixon, "Knowing that plants contain nutrients that can slow down and impede the cancer process is pretty motivating. Every time you put a healthy plant food on your plate, you'll feel good knowing you're giving your body the tools to keep cancer at bay."

She concludes, "And it doesn't hurt that these same foods help prevent other diseases as well. For preventing heart disease, diabetes, stroke, high blood pressure, arthritis, you name it—plants in the diet are nothing but helpful."

For more information or to read the full article, visit www.appleboost.com/newsletters/2010/01/26/how-to-turn-off-the-cancer-switch/.

# # #

Nutrition Intelligence Report, a free natural health and nutrition newsletter, is a publication of AppleBoost Products, Inc. For more information or past issues, or to sign up for a free subscription, visit www.appleboost.com/.

N: Network (Social) Communities and Social Bookmarking Sites

This example shows the original article and its repurposed use as a "News" and "Discussion" upload to a targeted group within LinkedIn.com. Modifications include a revised headline that would be more newsworthy and appealing to the target audience within this channel, including cutting down the article to an excerpt, synopsis, or "blurb" using the original first and fifth paragraphs, again, because I thought this was most appealing to target reader. Also added were a call to action and back-link for users to click through to read the original article.

SONAR Channel: Network (Social) Social Community

Source: LinkedIn.com (group: nutritional therapy)

====================

Turning Off Cancer? How Nutrition May Thwart Cancer Development

In the world of medical fears, few things rank as high as cancer. Fortunately, many cancers are curable.

Putting Plants to Work for You: Knowing that plants contain nutrients that can slow down and impede the cancer process is pretty motivating. Every time you put a healthy plant food on your plate, you'll feel good knowing you're giving your body the tools to keep cancer at bay. What do you think?

To read the full article, visit www.appleboost.com/newsletters/2010/01/26/how-to-turn-off-the-cancer-switch/.

==================

This example shows how the original article was repurposed for a social bookmarking site, where word limitations are prevalent. Modifications include the title, making it powerful and universally appealing to targeted readers within this platform. Other modifications include adding excerpts of the first and fifth paragraphs, as they encompass the main article well. I also added a call to action and back-link for readers to read the full article.

SONAR Channel: Social Bookmarking Site

Source: StumbleUpon.com

==================

www.appleboost.com/newsletters/2010/01/26/how-to-t...
How to Turn Off the Cancer Switch: How Nutrition Can Thwart Three Steps of Cancer Development

In the world of medical fears, few things rank as high as cancer. For many people, a cancer diagnosis challenges their view of themselves as a "healthy person." Fortunately, many cancers are curable. You can survive cancer and be healthy.

Putting Plants to Work for You

Knowing that plants contain nutrients that can slow down and impede the cancer process is pretty motivating. Every time you put a healthy plant food on your plate, you'll feel good knowing you're giving your body the tools to keep cancer at bay.

For the full article, visit appleboost.com/newsletters/2010/01/26/how-to-turn-off-the-cancer-switch/ [appleboost.com].

A: Article Directories

This example shows how the original article was repurposed for a niche article directory. Title remained the same, as it's extremely powerful and appealing to the targeted readers within this directory. Modifications include removing approximately five irrelevant words, as well as not including article references and footnotes that were on the original article's web page. I added an author's bio and back-link for readers to get more information or sign up to the e-newsletter.

SONAR Channel: Article Directory

Source: SelfGrowth.com

===================

How to Turn Off the Cancer Switch

By Suzanne Dixon

In the world of medical fears, few things rank as high as cancer. For many people, a cancer diagnosis challenges their view of themselves as a "healthy person." Fortunately, many cancers are curable. You can survive cancer and be healthy.

Cancer Biology 101

A basic understanding of how cancer develops can help you take advantage of what nutrition has to offer. Food can and should be a part of your plan for reducing the risk of cancer, and the risk of getting cancer again if you've already had it.

There are three basic steps to cancer development. Obviously, the process is very complicated at the cellular level. But the three-step model explains the most important changes that lead to cancer. These three steps represent some of the best opportunities for preventing cancer from developing at all.

Don't Be Initiated into This Club

The first step in cancer development is called initiation. One of the most common causes of initiation is free radical damage. Free radicals, which also go by the name oxidants, cause cell damage. Have you ever really thought about antioxidants? What is an oxidant? And why are we anti, or against, oxidants?

Oxidants cause oxidation, which is damaging to DNA—the instructions that tell cells what to do when. To wrap your head around oxidation, think of rusting.

Rusting is oxidation in the environment. Metal rusts, and it no longer functions as it should. This same process happens in the body. We don't exactly rust, but we do experience the same type of oxidation damage in our bodies.

This is where nutrition comes in. Vegetables, fruit, whole grains, legumes, nuts, and seeds—plant foods—are loaded with antioxidants. And not just the common antioxidants we all know and love. Beyond vitamin C, vitamin E, and beta-carotene are hundreds, even thousands of antioxidants in plant foods.

It's these thousands of antioxidants that work together to prevent oxidation in our bodies. In this very direct way, antioxidants in food prevent initiation. This is one of the ways by which plant foods are believed to reduce cancer risk.

But even with this plant protection, a few cells in our bodies are likely to be damaged, or initiated. The key to preventing cancer development also lies with the next step, called promotion.

One Promotion You Don't Want

The second step of the cancer-development process, called promotion, doesn't happen to just any cell. It happens to cells that already are initiated. We know plant foods limit the number of initiated cells, but what happens to the few cells that slip through the cracks?

Ideally, if a cell becomes damaged, it goes through a programmed cell death. This prevents it from multiplying and creating more damaged cells. However, for cells that are initiated but don't die, promotion, or step 2, can occur.

In promotion, damaged cells ignore the chemical messages of the normal cells around them. The damaged cell might be getting ready to multiply and grow. The normal cells in the neighborhood send chemical messages to prevent this. These messages say, "Stop, wait, don't go there." Promotion allows damaged cells to tune out the "stop" messages.

Here's where plant foods come to the rescue again. Among the thousands of nutrients found in plants are many that can help damaged cells hear the messages. These nutrients can, quite literally, act as little messengers. They make damaged cells sit up and take notice.

Dark purple and red foods seem to be especially adept at improving cellular communication. Think blackberries, blueberries, dark red cherries, grape juice, and red wine. Soy foods, such as tofu and tempeh, often touted for their possible effects on regulating female hormones (such as estrogen), have some antipromotion tricks up their sleeves as well.

And promotion is reversible. It's one of the only parts of cancer development that can actually be turned back! Plant foods can help a "deaf" cell hear again. In a sense, this can help a damaged cell become closer to normal.

Stop This Progress If You Can

This brings us to progression, the third step in cancer development. In progression, damaged cells take the communication problem one step further. Now these cells not only ignore messages; they begin to create their own messages. They try to influence the cells around them. It's like negative peer pressure.

This is the damaged cells' attempt to get normal cells to cooperate so they can grow and spread beyond the original site of cancer. This step is a key to metastasis—when cancer cells spread to distant parts of the body. This is important because it's only after cancer cells have spread that treating cancer becomes so difficult.

You guessed it. Plant foods have a role to play in blocking progression, too. Just as the thousands of naturally occurring phytonutrients in plants help damaged cells hear, they also help block unhealthy messages from damaged cells.

Many plant nutrients can act as roadblocks of a sort. They make it harder for damaged cells to influence the cells around them to misbehave, too. Several nutrients have been studied for their effects on preventing or slowing progression.

Resveratrol, found in red wine and grape juice; lycopene, found in cooked tomatoes, watermelon, and pink grapefruit; and quercetin, found in apples, tea, and onions, all seem particularly well suited for minimizing cancer cells' ability to go through the progression phase of cancer development.

Putting Plants to Work for You

Knowing that plants contain nutrients that can slow down and impede the cancer process is pretty motivating. Every time you put a healthy plant food on your plate, you'll feel good knowing you're giving your body the tools to keep cancer at bay.

And it doesn't hurt that these same foods help prevent other diseases as well. For preventing heart disease, diabetes, stroke, high blood pressure, arthritis, you name it—plants in the diet are nothing but helpful.

Every chance you get, throw in a plant food. You'll be on your way to better health.

Blueberries on your oatmeal? Check. Apple with lunch? Check. Nuts in your afternoon yogurt? Check. Carrots and hummus as a snack while fixing dinner? Check. A heaping pile of veggies with dinner? Check. Green leafies on your sandwich? Check.

The options are endless. The choice is up to you.

Author's Bio

Suzanne Dixon, MPH, MS, RD, is an internationally recognized expert in nutrition, chronic disease, cancer, and health and wellness, and the executive editor of *Nutrition Intelligence Report*, a free natural health and nutrition newsletter. For more information or past issues, or to sign up for a free subscription, visit www.appleboost.com/.

R: Relevant Posts to Blogs, Forums, Chat Rooms, and Message Boards

This example shows the repurposed article in a popular form, within a specialized category (relevant to the post's content). Modifications include a revised headline that would be appealing to targeted reader. Other revisions include repurposing content from paragraphs one and five of the original article to the form of a question (to encourage reader engagement). I also added a call to action and back-link for the reader to read the full article.

SONAR Channel: Relevant Post to Forum

Source: Topix.com

==================

Turn Off the Cancer Switch?: 3 Ways Nutrition May Thwart Cancer Development

Posted in the Health Forum

In the world of medical fears, few things rank as high as cancer. For many people, a cancer diagnosis challenges their view of themselves as a "healthy person." Fortunately, many cancers are curable. You can survive cancer and be healthy.

Knowing that plants contain nutrients that can slow down and impede the cancer process is pretty motivating. Every time you put a healthy plant food on your plate, you'll feel good knowing you're giving your body the tools to keep cancer at bay.

Do you agree?

For more details, check out www.appleboost.com/newsletters/2010/01....

SONAR Observations

One thing you might have noticed when reviewing the many recycled uses of the "Cancer Switch" article is that, in most instances, content was sliced, diced, and repurposed—from an article, to a press release, to a social media nugget, to interactive posts. Some popular methods of repurposing original article content include the following:

- Moving around or breaking up paragraphs
- Removing un-needed words (still leaving the integrity of the original article)
- Changing headlines or subheadings
- Adding a new call to action
- Adding a new closing paragraph
- Asking for reader participation

- Turning editorial content into quotes (for a press release)

- Shortening the spin-off article's length (turning it into a "blurb," excerpt, summary, or synopsis)

The constant factor is that all the uses stemmed from one original article. As I mentioned earlier, it's just a matter of looking at the content creatively and strategically—that vantage point will help you not only develop relevant content, but also determine targeted locations to upload it.

Does Your Content Have "Legs"?

You can identify who has picked up your content and republished it, see whether it went viral, and find back-links you've gotten from your efforts. I cover measurement details and analytics in Chapter 9, "Monetize Traffic: Blueprint to Building a Site That Leverages SONAR."

However, you can use a quick and easy way to measure the effects of your SONAR efforts on your visibility in organic search results.

A fast way to view some syndication and back-links is to search for the title of the article (and the author) in a top search engine, such as Google, Yahoo!, or Bing. The results will appear in the organic search listings (typically on the left side of the page) and show the syndication of the article—that is, if it's had "legs," where it's been republished.

Using this search process, here are just some of the examples for SONAR search results I found for the "Cancer Switch" article previously discussed:

AppleBoost—Newsletters » Blog Archive » Issue #8 : How To Turn ...

January 26, 2010 ... January 26th, 2010. Issue #8 : How To Turn Off The Cancer Switch. How Nutrition Can Thwart Three Steps of Cancer Development ...www.appleboost.com/.../2010/.../how-to-turn-off-the-cancer-switch/ - Cached

*Note: This is the original source article.

Believing This Could Raise Your Cancer Risk

April 20, 2010—Suzanne Dixon, MPH, MS, RD—Suzanne just wants everyone to be healthy. How to Turn Off the Cancer Switch—Alternative Health Aids For ....

ezinearticles.com/?Believing-This-Could-Raise-Your-Cancer... - Cached

How to Turn Off the Cancer Switch

March 12, 2010—Suzanne Dixon, MPH, MS, RD, is an internationally recognized expert in nutrition, chronic disease, cancer, ... See "Laetrile Case Histories," by Richardson, MD, and Griffin ... Nutrition Intelligence Report ....

www.healthiertalk.com/how-turn-cancer-switch-1422 - Cached

American Chronicle | How to Turn Off the Cancer Switch

How to Turn Off the Cancer Switch. Wendy Montes de Oca. January 29, 2010. In the world of medical fears, few things rank as high as cancer ....

www.americanchronicle.com/articles/view/138538 - Cached

How to Turn Off the Cancer Switch

February 23, 2010—A basic understanding of how cancer develops can help you take advantage of what nutrition has to offer. Food can and should be a part of....

www.articlesbase.com/cancer.../how-to-turn-off-the-cancer-switch-1896258.html - Cached

Superfoods Articles

How to Turn Off the Cancer Switch—by Suzanne Dixon. Submitted on January 26, 2010, from Wendy Montes de Oca. In the world of medical fears, few things rank as....

www.selfgrowth.com/superfoods_articles.html - Cached

How to Turn Off the Cancer Switch: Putting Plants to Work for You ...

Oct. 13, 2010 ... Knowing that plants contain nutrients that can slow down and impede the **cancer** process is pretty motivating. Every time you put a healthy ...
digg.com/news/...turn_off_the_cancer_switch.../who_dugg - Cached

Turn Off the Cancer Switch?: 3 Ways Nutrition May Thwart Cancer ...

2 posts - 1 author - Last post: Oct. 13, 2010

Oct. 13, 2010. *Turn Off The Cancer Switch?: 3 Ways Nutrition May Thwart Cancer Development.* Tell me when this thread is updated! ...
www.topix.com/forum/health/TCO974CSTATP53NJ8 - Cached

How to Turn Off the Cancer Switch

Feb. 1, 2010 ... How To *Turn Off The Cancer Switch*. How *Nutrition* Can *Thwart Three* Steps of ... How *Nutrition* Can *Thwart Three* Steps of *Cancer Development* ...
www.prlog.org/10514446-how-to-turn-off-the-cancer-switch.html

How to Turn Off the Cancer Switch

Feb. 17, 2010 ... How To Turn Off The Cancer Switch. How Nutrition Can Thwart Three Steps of Cancer Development. Email Contact Email PDF Version ...
www.prweb.com/releases/2010/02/prweb3584674.htm - Cached

Food - Churubusco - New York - United States - Latest News (Press ...

How To Turn Off The Cancer Switch. 1 year ago, 283 views, By Wendy Montes de Oca, MBA. How *Nutrition Can Thwart Three Steps of Cancer Development* ...
www.prlog.org/us,new-york,churubusco/cat-food/ - Cached

Diet and Nutrition - New York - United States - Latest News (Press ...

How To Turn Off The Cancer Switch. 11 months ago, By Wendy Montes de Oca, MBA. How *Nutrition Can Thwart Three Steps of Cancer Development* ...
www.prlog.org/us,new-york/tag-diet,nutrition/ - Cached

How to Turn Off the Cancer Switch - cancer development, cancer ...

4 posts - 1 author

How *Nutrition Can Thwart Three Steps of Cancer Development*. ... How *To Turn Off The Cancer Switch*. February 1, 2010. 8. How *Nutrition Can Thwart Three Steps* ...
www.free-press-release.com/news-how-to-turn-off-the-cancer-switch-1265065027.html - Cached

The results will show both SONAR and viral listings—where you've manually distributed the content, and the locations for which you didn't upload to but instead republished the content virally. In your weekly SONAR efforts, you'll typically upload to the same SONAR platforms, so any new sites that appear in results listings will be obvious.

Some examples of viral search results for the "Cancer Switch" article include these:

How to Turn Off the Cancer Switch—Cancer Resource—Stay...

May 27, 2010—In the world of medical fears, few things rank as high as cancer. *For many people, a* cancer *diagnosis challenges their view of themselves as....*

cancerblogs.info/how-to-turn-off-the-cancer-switch/ - Cached

How to Turn Off the Cancer Switch | Isons Nursery

October 3, 2010—How to Turn Off the Cancer Switch—In the world of medical fears, ... Suzanne Dixon, *MPH, MS, RD, is an internationally recognized expert in....*

www.isonsvineyards.com/.../how-to-turn-off-the-cancer-switch - Cached

How to Turn Off the Cancer Switch | Arthritis Helps

How To Turn Off The Cancer Switch. Churubusco, NY (PRWEB) February 17, 2010. In the world of medical fears, few things rank as high as cancer. ...
arthritishelps.com/14848/how-to-turn-off-the-cancer-switch/ - Cached

How to Turn Off the Cancer Switch | Cancer | Health News Articles

Aug. 1, 2010 ... In the world of medical fears, few things rank as high as *cancer.* For many people, a *cancer* diagnosis challenges their view of themselves as ...
www.healthtotalcare.com/how-to-turn-off-the-cancer-switch/ - Cached

carlton-branch: 11/10/08

Nov. 10, 2008 ... *How To Turn Off The Cancer Switch. How To Turn Off The Cancer Switch.* How *Nutrition Can Thwart Three Steps of Cancer Development ...*
carlton-branch.blogspot.com/2008_11_10_archive.html - Cached

SONAR Takeaways

I've found that SONAR works best when it's part of a weekly routine, or a system within a system, so you can block out that time on your schedule accordingly. This means you need to spend two to four hours per week repurposing content and disseminating it throughout the Web via the five SONAR platforms.

Although the best days for press release distribution are typically Tuesday through Thursday, you can deploy SONAR tactics any day of the week and adjust it to your own schedule and workload. However, I highly recommend keeping it the same day every week—ideally the same day your e-zine goes live and as close as possible to the time of its release—to ride the wave of natural momentum from your e-zine circulation as well as create additional organic traction and buzz on the Web … this timing—close proximity of SONAR distribution to the original content going live—is the cornerstone of the entire SONAR Content Distribution Model's™ power.

The more you do it, the less time it will take you every week.

Five critical elements contribute to SONAR success:

- **Synchronization is key**—Release your content into the five SONAR channels within the same 24-hour period as you release the source content (your e-zine or blog post). This should be as close as possible to the original content's release. The timeliness of the content's release from multiple web platforms at once creates a surge of volume, awareness, and buzz within each respective network and drives traffic to your website. If efforts are fragmented, and some are done one day, and some another—it will break the organic "momentum" and in turn affect the content's listing (page rank) in the organic search results. Your goal is to get the most traction and leverage from your main article.

- **Be both a creative and a strategic thinker**—Repurpose your content, know where to disseminate it, and know how to make others want to read it is essential. Take your article source and make minor "tweaks" to the headline, intro paragraph, or closing paragraph so it's slightly different in each location you upload it to. Or, upload different lengths of article excerpts in each SONAR channel. The goal is to keep the integrity of the article with minor edits.

- **Link, link, link**—Don't forget to add a link in your content. This is actually beneficial to your SEO/SEM efforts and driving traffic to your main website. The links can be in the body content (that is, "for more information, visit *www.yourarticlenewsletterarhicvepage.com*") or in the author's bio section. This also plays an important role with content syndication, as whatever site or blog reposts your content, is another relevant site that will be giving your site "link juice." Note: The rules of link placement will vary in each SONAR platform, so place links accordingly.

- **Keyword selection**—It's important to use targeted, researched keywords in headlines, subheads, body content, and tags (each platform may ask for "tags" or "keywords" when uploading content). This consistency will help with your organic listing placement.

- **The results**—If done correctly (timing, frequency, keywords, and so
  on), SONAR content will appear under targeted keyword search terms
  on a weekly basis and dominate those keyword search terms in the
  organic search listings pages 1–3, thereby creating buzz, visibility, brand
  exposure, and traffic generation to your website.

In my experience, if you add these techniques to your online marketing mix and
optimize your website to harness the traffic, they will dramatically affect your web
traffic and prospecting.

SONAR AND WORDPRESS

When setting up your content management system for online publishing, it's
important to pick a system that is friendly to both users and search engines.
Many webmasters prefer WordPress for its ease of use and manageability. In
addition, search engines prefer URLs that have the keywords as part of the
web address. WordPress fosters this process. Ideally, the URL should include
the website name and then the article title or descriptive text that is keyword
dense.

A good example of a keyword-rich URL is www.appleboost.com/
newsletters/2010/01/26/how-to-turn-off-the-cancer-switch/.

7

SEO for SONAR: How to Get Found by Search Engines

As mentioned earlier in the book, keyword selection is critical when doing article marketing. And the same keyword tools and research that you use in article marketing—such as Google Keyword External Tool, WordTracker, and KeyWordDiscovery—you can also use to identify your keywords for SONAR marketing.

After conducting your research, you should format the content with the most keyword density, in descending order:

Headline

Subheadline or introduction copy

Body text, including body subheadings (if any)

Closing or call to action

Author bio

If a URL (web address link to the main article) can be added either within the body content or in the author's section, the best URL formats are those that also have keywords in the address that are related to the headline. See the example in Chapter 6, "Learning and Leveraging the SONAR Content Distribution Model," in the "Cancer Switch" article. In a nutshell, the goal is to incorporate some of your primary keywords into your URL, perhaps the article's headline, such as the "...how-to-turn-off-the-cancer-switch/" in the URL, "www.appleboost.com/newsletters/2010/01/26/how-to-turn-off-the-cancer-switch/." This is important because one of the factors that influences page rank in the organic search results listing are web pages that have their keywords as part of the actual URL.

> ...the goal is to incorporate some of your primary keywords into your URL.

Because the center of your content distribution wheel (see Figure 6.1) is the original content, after you do your initial article repurposing and keyword adoption for the article being used in the article directories (the *A* in SONAR), you don't need to do much, if any, additional keyword research for the remaining uses of the content and the related distribution platforms.

Start with your syndicate partners and work your way out, reusing the content for the other distribution channels (see Figure 7.1). Follow these steps:

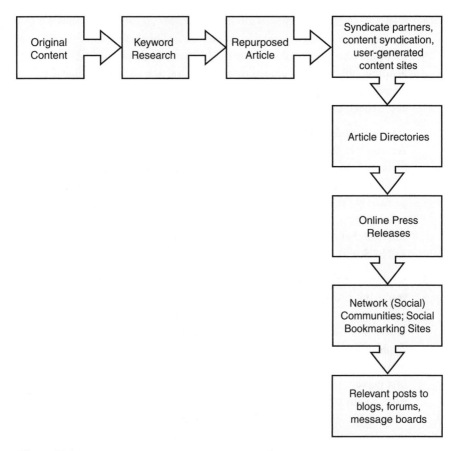

Figure 7.1 *SONAR content distribution process flow*

Although SONAR can be used in most any order and still be effective, the following illustration is a suggested process flow:

1. Step 1: Start with your original article or "original source" content.

2. Step 2: Conduct your primary keyword research. The keywords from the original content will primarily be the same as the original source content becomes repurposed and will pass through to all your SONAR distribution channels.

3. Step 3: Your first repurposed article is for syndicate partners, content syndication, and user-generated content sites. For these uses, it's a matter of making minor edits to original content—perhaps modifying headline, subheads, or uploading a shorter versions or the original article such as excerpts or blurbs. Don't forget to add your call to action and to back-link to original article source.

4. Step 4: Your repurposed article can then be used and slightly modified even further for submission to article directories. Again, this can involve minor modifications including the aforementioned as well as moving around paragraphs or removing unnecessary words that aren't germane to the article. As with the previous step, it's important to add your call to action and to back-link to your website. In this step, you will find that most article directories allow you to add a call to action and back-link in the author's bio or custom auto-signature fields.

5. Step 5: With the online press release distribution channel, even though you're not simply uploading an article to a free online PR site, you do need a base article—a foundation—and that's your initial repurposed article. The next step is to spin that foundation into a press release. To do this effectively, you need to have a fundamental knowledge of basic press release format: layout, writing style (in third person as opposed to first person), and strong quotes mixed with body copy. Tell a short story—with a beginning, middle, and end—that is newsworthy. And as with all of the repurposed content, make sure to include your back-link. This can be done in the body of the actual release, such as "For more information visit…" or in the "About Us" section of the release.

6. Step 6: After you repurpose your original content as a press release, make sure most of your original primary keywords are still intact. Also, when you think of your headline and subheadline for the release and the quotes in the body copy, be sure to include your primary keywords. When proofreading your release, look at in terms of human readers as well as search engines. Pay attention to the keywords being used and the density from the top of the page to the bottom—the top of the page should be more keyword rich. Having some redundancy in keywords is okay as long as the overall release is newsworthy and informative to bloggers, online news aggregators (such as Yahoo! News or Google News), media outlets, online journalists, and consumers.

Note

Although each online press release website has its own built-in template via an online form, it's unwise to work directly in the template. Instead, I recommend creating and storing your final release in a Word document. Then you can simply copy and paste material from the Word document to the website fields as needed.

7. Step 7: Next, you can take excerpts or blurbs from either your main article or press release and upload them to network (social) communities and social bookmarking sites. Since social communities often employ character count maximums, it's most important to be judicious with the limited space you have to work with. Make sure the headline and brief descriptive text is captivating and appealing to each community's target audience. Also, make sure to include a back-link to the main source article.

8. Step 8: Finally, you can repurpose content from your main article or press release and use it in targeted blogs, forums and message boards. This part of the process takes the most finesse and creativity. You also need to abide by each site's rules and guidelines (that is, protocol, back-linking) as well as the basic strategies discussed in Chapter 4 ("What Came First: The Guerrilla or the Web") and Chapter 6 ("Learning and Leveraging the SONAR Content Distribution Model™") regarding uploading relevant, useful, actionable, and informative posts that are not blatant spam messages.

Creating press releases for many who are unfamiliar with the basic formatting may involve a learning curve. To help expedite this process, I've included some real-life examples.

The following examples are press releases that I've created for myself or for some of my clients. You might find them to be helpful as a guide to creating your own online press releases.

 Note

These websites also contain some great information and online press release samples:

- http://blog.prleap.com/archives/sample-press-release-format/
- www.businesswire.com/portal/site/home/sample-press-release/
- http://service.prweb.com/learning/c/release-ideas/

Business Services/Marketing Example

Note how the following keywords are used in the headline, subheadline, and body copy.

Keywords: marketing, media, search engine marketing, social media, PR, direct marketing, multichannel marketing, pay-per-click, PR, publishing, leads, revenues, optimization, Wendy Montes de Oca, branding, Web 2.0, online marketing, marketing professionals, marketing consulting, small business owners, and entrepreneurs.

Keyword density should be heaviest from top to bottom of the page. Again, in a release, it's OK to be somewhat repetitive as long as it's newsworthy and relevant. Also note the call to action and "About" section.

Precision Marketing and Media Announces Launch of Website and Provides Powerful Marketing Solutions

During such turbulent times, when companies are struggling to bring in customers, Precision Marketing and Media is providing proven search engine marketing, social media, PR, and direct marketing tactics to help clients increase revenues.

FOR IMMEDIATE RELEASE

*PRLog (Press Release)—April 20, 2009—*During such turbulent times, when companies, marketing professionals, small business owners, and entrepreneurs are struggling to bring in new (and keep existing) customers, Precision Marketing and Media, LLC, is providing proven search engine marketing, optimization, social media, pay-per-click, PR, publishing, and direct marketing tactics to help clients build market share, generate leads, and increase revenues.

According to president and founder Wendy Montes de Oca, MBA, "I am thrilled to have officially launched the business ... and the website ... to such promising results. I'm flattered and, quite frankly, honored to get such terrific response from respected industry colleagues and new clients. It's more than I could have hoped for."

When asked what makes her company different from other marketing consulting agencies, Montes de Oca added, "It's a tough time right now. Business owners are looking for cost-effective ways to bring in new customers, get more traffic to their website, and increase sales ... and they want it all at a reasonable cost. We are creative, strategic thinkers that get results and stretch the clients' marketing dollars."

She continues, "Most agencies are not direct response experts; they focus on branding or general marketing. They don't know how to leverage Web 2.0 platforms such as social media or user-generated content sites (such as Digg). My company provides multichannel marketing solutions specializing in online efforts. It's a complete one-stop shop."

Montes de Oca concluded, "I have over 16 years of multichannel and direct response marketing experience under my belt, and I've led the marketing efforts for Fortune 500 companies and top publishers. I not only talk the talk, but I also walk the walk. Now it's time for me to finally share the skills I've honed over the years with others. I'm really looking forward to helping businesses flourish, especially during this economic hardship. That's what makes it all worthwhile!"

For more information or press inquiries, please visit www.precisionmarketingmedia.com/.

About Precision Marketing and Media, LLC

Precision Marketing and Media was founded in 2009 by multichannel marketing expert and media maven Wendy Montes de Oca, MBA. Precision Marketing and Media, LLC, provides powerful and proven real-world strategies for optimizing and monetizing business-to-business (B2B) or business-to-consumer (B2C) business efforts, including direct response marketing, direct mail, email, online marketing, list building, content syndication, search engine optimization (SEO), search engine marketing (SEM), social media optimization (SMO), pay-per-click (PPC), grass roots marketing, multichannel marketing, online PR, media buying, affiliate marketing, new product launches, business development, and more.

Alternative Health/Health Publishing Example

Note once again that the keywords are used in the headline, subheadline, and body copy. Keyword density should be heaviest from top to bottom. Also note the call to action prompting reader to click through for more information or to sign up for the free enewsletter.

Keywords: apple(s), appleboost, apple peel, apple peel powder, nutrition, an apple a day, nutritional, nutrients, nature, free health newsletter, health, healthy, good health, healthful properties, certified organic apples, high-fiber, low-calorie, antioxidant, phytonutrient, medical, ailments, cancer, diabetes, heart disease, arthritis, high cholesterol, inflammation, Parkinson's, Alzheimer's, and respiratory illnesses.

AppleBoost.com Launches New Website: Harnessing the Nutrition and Health Benefits of Organic Apples with Breakthrough Dried Apple Peel Powder

AppleBoost Products, Inc., has taken the adage, "An apple a day keeps the doctor away" to a whole new level with its groundbreaking, patented dried apple peel powder (DAPP), which harnesses the many nutritional properties of this high-fiber, low-calorie, antioxidant- and phytonutrient-rich fruit, and makes it fun to enjoy.

Churubusco, NY (PRWEB)—November 10, 2009

Many people have heard the old saying, "An apple a day keeps the doctor away." Well, there's something to that. Medical studies suggest that apples and apple peel may be beneficial in reducing many common ailments that can include cancer, diabetes, heart disease, arthritis, high cholesterol, inflammation, Parkinson's, Alzheimer's, and respiratory illnesses.

AppleBoost Products, Inc., has taken the adage to a whole new level with its groundbreaking, patented dried apple peel powder (DAPP), which harnesses the many nutritional properties of this high-fiber, low-calorie, antioxidant- and phytonutrient-rich fruit, and makes it fun to enjoy.

Now it's easier than ever to learn about the power of apples, with AppleBoost.com's new website that is consumer friendly and features not only AppleBoost's unique product line (which utilizes only the freshest, certified organic apples that are free of chemical pesticides, artificial fertilizers, and ionizing radiation), but also contains healthy recipes, informative articles, educational information, a free health newsletter *(Nutrition Intelligence Report)*, a health glossary, and much more.

According to Dave Copeland, president of AppleBoost Products, Inc., "We're thrilled to launch the new site and help take the nutritional benefits of this magnificent fruit to the masses in a tasty, economic, and convenient way."

Copeland adds, "With people's hectic schedules, it's not always realistic to consume the amount of apples needed to do the body good. But we've changed that with our energy tubes, powders, and capsules … perfect for just about everyone … from mothers, to kids, to seniors, to people on the go. No one should miss out on the opportunity for good health."

It was in the laboratories at Cornell University's Department of Food Science that apple peel's healthful properties were first unlocked. Leading researcher Rui Hai Liu, Ph.D., focused much of his research on extracting the maximum nutritional value out of fruits and vegetables. His research led him to develop a patented process for drying and milling apple peel (which concentrates even further the already-dense nutrients in apple peel).

Copeland concluded, "AppleBoost has taken what Mother Nature perfected and simply turned it into a total package … and without any chemical alternations. We're proud to bring this amazing breakthrough to consumers nationwide."

For more information or to sign up for the free health newsletter, *Nutrition Intelligence Report*, visit www.appleboost.com/.

# # #

Business Services/Marketing/InfoPublishing Example

Note that you can see how keywords are used in the headline, subheadline, and body copy. Also note the call to action and "About" section.

Keywords: recession-proof strategies, growing profits, soft economy, Bob Bly, increasing sales, business strategies, leverage customers, business owners, income generating, entrepreneurs, marketers, marketing, and revenue.

New Report Offers Powerful Recession-Proof Strategies for Growing Profits During a Soft Economy

During a time when the nation is struggling and business are shutting down, a new report from best-selling author and marketing strategist Bob Bly offers powerful solutions for increasing bottom-line sales and leveraging existing customers.

FOR IMMEDIATE RELEASE

*PRLog (Press Release)—April 15, 2009—*During a time when the nation is struggling—business are shutting down, jobs are getting cut, and houses are getting foreclosed—a new report from best-selling author and marketing strategist Bob Bly titled "Recession-Proof Business Strategies: 15 Winning Methods to Sell Any Product or Service in a Down Economy" offers proven and powerful solutions for increasing bottom-line sales and leveraging existing customers.

According to Bly, "It doesn't take a recession to create problems for a business. The current situation is just magnifying the problem. Business owners need to develop core income-generating solutions that succeed when times are tough."

He added, "What follows are some powerful strategies that will help business owners large and small, as well as entrepreneurs and marketers, increase sales while their competition is fighting to stay afloat."

Here are Bly's top three tips to generate cash during a soft economy:

1. Use low-cost "add-ons" to generate additional revenue. In other words, bundle your products or services. According to Bly, "If one of my clients has hired me to write a sales letter for a new product, chances are, they'll want a press release to promote that product. Adding on this service provides value to the client, and the additional cost is incremental."

2. Repackage your services to accommodate smaller customers or reduced budgets. "In my consulting business," Bly said, "if a client cannot pay, let's say, $5,000 for me to write him a direct mail package, I may critique a package the client actually wrote for $500." This method can be applied across the board. For manufacturers, it could be a no-frills offer or compact version of an existing product. It could also be smaller order requirements, extended payment plans, or special discount incentives.

3. Add value to your existing products or services. Businesses can win new customers by offering faster delivery, a larger product selection than the competition, easier payment terms, or a more attractive guarantee or refund policy. According to Bly, "These little extras always pay big dividends and provide goodwill to current and new customers."

Bly concluded, "Recessions do not last forever. Historically, they have lasted anywhere from 12 to 17 months. Don't despair. If you follow all my strategies, it is possible for your business to become busy and, more importantly, profitable again."

For the full list of winning recession-proof strategies, please visit www.bly.com or www.bly.com/recessionsurvey.

About Bob Bly

Best-selling author, marketing strategist, copywriter, and consultant Bob Bly has more than 25 years of business and direct response marketing experience. Bly's clients include Fortune 500 companies and some of the country's leading publishers. He is the author of more than 70 books and is a distinguished speaker and editorial contributor to prominent publications and associations, including DMNews, Target Marketing, the Specialized Information Publisher's Association (SIPA), and more. His popular free newsletter, *The Direct Response Letter*, has nearly 100,000 subscribers and contains "insider secrets" to double response rates, generate more leads and orders, and help your marketing make more money.

For more information or press inquiries, please contact Wendy Montes de Oca, MBA, at media@precisionmarketingmedia.com.

Business Services/Self-Help/Professional and Personal Development Example

Here, you can see another example of keyword density is used from the top of the page to the bottom (headline, subheadline, and body). Also note the "About" section, which contains the call to action and back-link and mention about free newsletter sign up.

Keywords: leadership skills, Karen Keller, Karen Keller, Ph.D., Dr. Karen Keller, Karen-Keller.com, influence expert, women leadership, persuasion skills, success, influence skills, women and business, executive education, women education, women empowerment, female empowerment, female leadership, women empowering women, women entrepreneurs, and free.

Learn the True Secrets of Female Leadership, Influence, Empowerment, and Success. Women: Transform Your Life Now, for Free

Women: Transform your life regarding money, career, health, family, and relationships ... now! Influence expert Dr. Karen Keller launches her new website, Karen-Keller.com, and free newsletter, Influence It!

Real Power for Women, *which empowers women to use influence and persuasion skills to master their lives.*

Fort Wayne, IN (PRWEB)—October 27, 2010

Influence expert Dr. Karen Keller launches her new website, Karen-Keller.com, and free newsletter, *Influence It! Real Power for Women,* which empowers women to use the art of influence and persuasion to discover, conquer, and master their lives.

According to Keller, who's known in the industry as the female Dale Carnegie, "Women possess many innate skills that guarantee excellence in everything they do. But oftentimes we second-guess ourselves in decisions, losing the leadership qualities that take our lives—personal or professional—to levels beyond our imagination."

She adds, "Influence is not a mystery. Learning (and knowing) how to influence a situation … a person … a decision … an outcome … or yourself … is a skill that can be mastered but first requires cultivation."

Dr. Keller, who developed the "Influence It!" principle, has for the last 25 years personally leveraged influence skills and its proven power for her own success in career, education, and home. She then became a sought-after coach, teaching her skills to business owners, Fortune 500 executives, and entrepreneurs to help transform careers and, ultimately, lives.

When asked what makes her approach unique, Keller replied, "Although many of my clients have been men, I've seen an overwhelming deficiency in the leadership and influence techniques geared toward women, as well as an absence of information on the Web. That's when I decided to fill this crucial void and focus my efforts on female empowerment, creating an information-packed, easy-to-use website, as well as an insightful newsletter. It's all to help empower women."

Keller concluded, "I am pouring my heart and soul into the newsletter and website (http://karen-keller.com/). There will be powerful, breakthrough, yet easy-to-implement information that all women can learn … and live … whether they're the matriarch of their home or nucleolus of their office. After all, a gal's gotta escape from her comfort zone to obtain the things she really wants out of life … personally or professionally … and the art of influence will definitely help accomplish that!"

About Dr. Keller

Karen Keller, Ph.D., is an expert in women's leadership and assertiveness training. She is also a successful entrepreneur and author. She specializes in the skills of influence and persuasion, executive coaching, mentoring, sales techniques, management development training, motivational speaking, personal life coaching, and corporate training. Discover *Influence It! Real Power for Women Now!*. For your free subscription, visit http://karen-keller.com/.

SEM for SONAR: How to Get Found by Search Engines

Although you can't control the behind-the-scenes meta tags within each SONAR platform to which you are distributing your content, you can control the relevance, density, and use of keywords within the content being repurposed.

Within most of the SONAR content distribution channels, you can also assign tags or keywords to the content within the article directory, social bookmarking, or press release site. Those tags are critical in search engine marketing (SEM). Within other locations, such as message boards, forums, blogs, and network communities, the location or subcategory in which you are posting your content helps categorize your content accordingly in the search engine results.

However, the most important page for optimization is your original content—the original article that everything else stems from and links to. The article that is housed in your newsletter archives on your website.

This webpage needs to have many elements for it to stand on its own for search engine marketing purposes and help get the best results for your SONAR efforts.

Consider these key elements when setting up the HTML for your original content:

- As mentioned in Chapter 6, it's a good idea to consider WordPress as your content-management system. WordPress is user-friendly and very compatible with search engines. It automatically generates links that are keyword rich. For most sites, it should be easy to install via a plug-in. Discuss this option with your webmaster (unless you are the webmaster or have web programming experience).

- If you don't have WordPress and are uploading articles manually to your website, make sure each article page has the following information:

- A title tag that contains up to 65 characters, has relevant keywords, and is unique to each article page.

- Headlines that are emphasized with H1or "header" tags (codes that are behind the scenes for the search engines to index).

- Meta descriptions that are keyword dense and reader-friendly. This is what will show up in organic search engine results listings. Length should be about 250 characters.

- Up to 25 relevant meta keywords per article page.

- Article images (alt tags) that are named using relevant keywords or phrases.

- Intrasite links within the body content of the article.

- Webpage name (URL) that is relevant to the keywords.

- Keywords within the article body that are emphasized (bolded, under-lined, or italicized).

- Remember that tags and keywords are optimal when they coincide with the actual content in the body of your article. Try to weave as many keywords as you can into your body text.

Helpful Hints for Writers When Working with Search Engines

In many organizations, large and small, you'll find two sets of departments—editorial and marketing. The two usually work with each other but don't commingle. But over the years, I've found that the most optimized articles—the ones that get traction and drive traffic back to the publisher's website—are the articles in which the editorial writers step outside their normal boundaries as they're writing their articles for the newsletter and keep search engines firmly in mind.

For die-hard writers or journalists, it might take some time to get used to this way of thinking and writing. But it does help streamline the entire web writing process and create the ideal article for both human readers and search engines.

When writers don't embrace this mindset, they might write a fantastic article, but the article isn't poised for maximum Internet distribution and traffic generation. The article likely contains typically little to no primary keywords in the headline, subheading, or body text. Then when the article gets posted to the website or blog, any search engine tagging is ineffective. This is a crucial mistake that directly impacts this article's visibility in the organic search results and fails to get the right target prospect to find it.

I offer these tips to writers:

- Write the article with an editorial mindset, incorporating basic writing techniques and your own personal style. This helps make the article unique to each writer's personality and nuisances, but it also incorporates classic journalistic qualities. This is your first draft.

- Carefully read through your first draft and incorporate your business's primary or core keywords (as defined by the marketing team) wherever possible—in the headline, subheads, and body text. Maintain the editorial integrity of the article, but enhance it from a search engine standpoint. Remember, you're ultimately writing for both human and search engine readers. This is your second draft.

- Ensure that the final article contains a blend of both editorial and search engine qualities. This is the best of both worlds. Your article now is ready to be posted on a website or blog. This is your third and final draft.

Continually work with your Internet marketers to make sure you understand the core keywords to emphasize in editorial writing.

> Remember, you're ultimately writing for both human and search engine readers.

8

SONAR in Action:
Results and Analytics

As mentioned earlier in this book, the SONAR Content Distribution Model™ isn't just theory; it's a proven, systematic strategy that has worked repeatedly across industries.

This chapter includes case studies to illustrate SONAR's effectiveness. The tactics used to reach the performance levels mentioned in the following case studies are the very ones mentioned throughout this book.

Although I'm not at liberty to share specific company names, I can highlight SONAR performance for a company's niche. I also can share details of my own company's SONAR performance.

This data is a compilation of my own tracking research and metrics using the tools I discuss in this chapter—such as the 3 Os, Google Analytics, and back-link checkers—as well as both anecdotal data and performance data provided to me by the companies and clients that I've worked for. To help organize the data, I sometimes used a Benchmark and Progression Chart.

The SONAR process, although efficient and effective, might seem daunting when you're first learning it—especially if you're not accustomed to working in a systematic, methodical manner. You may feel overwhelmed uploading your content to the various, targeted websites within the five SONAR distribution platforms—the same time frame, every week. However, based on my personal experience—actually implementing SONAR and training others to use SONAR—the learning curve is typically short (that is, a few weeks), and the results will be worth it.

It's important to keep things in perspective. Remember that the time you spend each week deploying these FREE tactics, and the results you will see, outweighs the time you spend employing SONAR tactics.

All of following results were achieved without spending any money on external advertising or related costs (such as media buys, list rentals, and so on).

Case Study #1

Business Niche: Professional Services

Company: Precision Marketing and Media, LLC

As part of my weekly SONAR marketing efforts, I uploaded content to several SONAR channels, including LinkedIn, Digg, StumbleUpon, and other social media, online PR, and top article directories—all in about an hour per week. For every one article from my blog that I repurposed and circulated in a relevant and targeted LinkedIn marketing group (via "Discussion" or "News" submissions), that article created interest, engaged readers, encouraged participation, and generated about five leads for my consulting services per week. That's five leads per group, per week, for a total of up to 25 leads per week with no out-of-pocket advertising costs. This occurred steadily for nearly two months, resulting in several consulting clients. Bottom line: Just one consulting client's monthly retainer covered time spent on my SONAR marketing efforts more than tenfold.

Case Study #2

Business Niche: Alternative Health

Company: Confidential

For one alternative health website, the SONAR Content Distribution Model™ helped produce the following results in three months:

- Increased organic page (traffic) ranking and visits by 3,160% and 81.5%, respectively, with no outside advertising tactics.
- Grew the list by more than 20,000 names.

- SONAR tactics were implemented by me directly, on average spending a total of about 2–4 hours per week. Because this was a bi-weekly publication, SONAR efforts culminated around the circulation dates of the e-newsletter.

Case Study #3

Business Niche: Financial

Company: Confidential

A popular finance and investing website achieved the following results after using SONAR marketing tactics for four months:

- Traffic visits increased by nearly 80%.

- Organic page (traffic) ranking increased by nearly 150%.

- And because the website had been set up to harness traffic (through select lead generation and sales elements, which I'll discuss more in Chapter 9), this surge in traffic was monetized for a return on investment (ROI) of 221%.

- SONAR tactics were implemented by me directly, on average spending a total of about 2–5 hours per week. Because this was a daily publication, I spent less than an hour per day on SONAR efforts after the e-newsletter went live.

Case Study #4

Business Niche: Alternative Health and Nutrition

Company: Confidential

For another health website, the following results were demonstrated six months after utilizing SONAR marketing tactics:

- List growth of nearly 35%.

- Total revenue growth year-over-year of nearly 50%.

- Total website traffic increase of nearly 110%.

- Six months' gross organic Internet sales of nearly $150,000 (with no outside advertising expense).

- Average SONAR time spent each week was approximately 1–2 hours and occurred the day the newsletter went live.

Case Study #5

Business Niche: Alternative Health and Nutrition

Company: Confidential

For this online website, the following milestones were achieved within 10 months of implementing SONAR strategies:

- List growth was five times larger than its initial list size.

- Organic Internet sales were 10 times more than in the previous two years combined.

- Website page (traffic) rank increased 1,300%.

- Average SONAR time spent each week was approximately 2 hours and occurred the day the newsletter went live.

Case Study #6

Business Niche: Professional Services

Company: Confidential

Just two weeks after deploying SONAR tactics, Google Analytics for this website displayed the following results:

- Average weekly visits more than doubled, for a total increase of 128.66%.

- Average weekly home page sign-ups (lead generation) increased more than four times.

- Alexa traffic rank increased 103% and 104% for global and U.S. scores, respectively.

- Sales increased nearly 700% from historical (lifetime) average.

- In addition, nearly four months after implementing SONAR, Alexa page (traffic) rank for domestic and global visits increased 164.82% and 143.36%, respectively, and organic lead generation increased 32.41% (net).

- Overall, year-over-year website visits were up 505.76%.

Note

> It's important to note in this particular scenario that the SONAR tactics for
> the most part were implemented by a third-party hired by the client. And
> for whatever reason unbeknownst to me and outside of my control, this
> third-party didn't deploy SONAR exactly as I had directed and trained them
> to do so (that is, frequency, recommended websites, timing, and rele-
> vance). So these results, although impressive and substantial, are still not
> the optimum results—they actually could have been higher.

Case Study #7

Business Niche: Professional Services

Company: Confidential

After implementing new social media and online marketing tactics, including
SONAR, one publisher reported a year-over-year increase of nearly 10,000 new
leads for that time period and a year-over-year sales increase of more than 25%.

- Average SONAR time spent each week was estimated to be 2–4 hours
  and occurred the day the newsletter went live. SONAR implementation
  was split between myself and a third-party the client hired. This third-
  party was unfamiliar with SEO, social media, and press release creation,
  so additional time was spent on training and work review as part of the
  learning curve.

Case Study #8

Business Niche: Health

Company: Confidential

Three months after implementing SONAR and other recommended Internet
marketing tactics, one online health publisher reported these results:

- An increase in e-newsletter subscribers of approximately 35%.

- Organic website traffic visits that more than doubled.

- Average SONAR time spent each week was approximately 2–4 hours
  and occurred the day the newsletter went live. SONAR implementation
  was split between me and an in-house staffer; therefore, extra time was
  needed for work review.

SONAR: Keeping It Real and Replicating Results

Did you ever get an email promotion with promises such as "Earn $10,000 in 10 hours," "Make $1 million a year on the Internet," or "Get 60,000 email addresses in just two months"?

These claims are usually marketing ploys that focus on a consumer's emotion and the greed factor. The claims could be completely false or could have some shred of truth behind them, but they're repositioned and spun in such a way that they're misleading—and nearly all the valid data is lost.

I'm always skeptical about such claims, and they often rub me the wrong way. Here's why:

Recently, a client said to me, "Susan is saying she's received 50,000 email addresses in about a month. And George sent an email saying he's made more than $50,000 in one day! How is that possible? Can we do something like this? Do you know how they did it?"

My initial thought reminded me of something I've heard since I was a kid: If it sounds too good to be true, it usually is. Then I paused, took a deep breath, and replied:

"As far as rapid list growth, you can't compare your average, run-of-the-mill start-up company with limited resources, limited leverage, and no network of contacts to a company that has an established online presence with access to lists or friends in the industry to help with cross-marketing and list-building efforts. You heard only half the story. These claims might be true, but in my experience, they're an anomaly. These are not the results your average start-up company can realistically obtain in such a short time span. So proceed with caution."

That's why I wholeheartedly believe in the SONAR Content Distribution Model™. It's real, it's proven, and it involves virtually no ancillary costs to deploy, so practically anyone can do it—companies large or small, start-up or established.

As long as someone has content, the SONAR system can be duplicated and replicated for their specific needs. Results will happen in a realistic time frame because SONAR's main objectives are to generate targeted, organic traffic, increase website visibility, and raise awareness or industry buzz—all without advertising costs. So, if you're looking for a "get rich quick" scheme, SONAR is not for you.

...if you're looking for a "get rich quick" scheme, SONAR is not for you.

How the website traffic SONAR generates is then monetized for profits depends on how well the website has been optimized and designed to harness traffic leads (email capture) and sales.

When you see one of those "too good to be true" email promotions or hear a somewhat unbelievable claim, ask yourself some rational questions that focus on the nuts and bolts behind the numbers:

- Where is this sales number coming from?

- What is the price per unit of what was sold and reported?

- How many total customers or orders were calculated into this figure?

- How many net sales, orders, or customers were there after factoring in cancels, returns, cost of goods sold, and advertising?

- How much was spent on advertising, marketing, or list rentals to make this sales number happen, and for how long?

- How frequently were these lists marketed to?

- How long has this person been running an online business: Is it a web "start-up" or "staple"?

- What is this person's web presence? Does this person have a long list of friends and colleagues to reach out to for promotional help, or is the person using organic methods?

You'll hear a lot of inflammatory claims, especially with Internet marketing products. Many of these claims don't give the reader the full and complete picture—they're giving only a strategic snapshot. If business owners or copywriters offer up some of the aforementioned considerations when footnoting their "claim," then at least they're attempting to be honest and present all the facts supporting their figures.

This makes me think of another cliché that I've heard since I was a kid, and it couldn't ring more true: Let the buyer beware.

Anytime you see or hear a claim that seems unbelievable, take it with a grain of salt, because there's more to it than meets the eye.

How Is SONAR Measured?

The SONAR Content Distribution Model™ incorporates many online marketing tactics: article marketing, online press releases, social media and bookmarking, and interactions with like-minded individuals in message boards or forums.

When you look at SONAR marketing, much of the tactics are search engine and social media related.

Many online marketers are deploying social and search engine marketing strategies but don't necessarily know how to quantify the results and measure them against their marketing budget, goals, and resources available.

To help measure my SONAR and social media and search engine marketing initiatives, I looked at the analytical data from three vantage points based on my real-life experience: Internet marketing, direct response, and PR. Because many of these core elements are in SONAR, the forms I used to measure each of these efforts separately are the same that I use for measuring SONAR. I call them the three Os—outputs, outcomes, and objectives.

The Three Os—Outputs, Outcomes, and Objectives

- **Outputs**—Measure effectiveness and efficiency, such as new subscriber sign-ups and spikes in website traffic during your campaign. Outputs also measure analytics, such as referring website sources, visits, unique visits, and visit percentages.

- **Outcomes**—Measure behavioral changes, such as internal customer and subscriber feedback (calls, emails, and forum postings) on your website, and external reputation monitoring or visits to targeted chat rooms during your campaign to see the buzz.

- **Objectives**—Compare direct product sales during the time of the campaign to other sales that occurred before the campaign. Objectives establish a baseline, giving room for sales assumptions tied to your effort.

Several free online tools can help track and quantify your SONAR and social media marketing efforts:

- **Google Analytics**—Check the Referring Sources page to see how much traffic was generated by the social media sites you've been active in. Look at overall traffic to the website during the same time period of your efforts. If you have a sign-up or email form, look for lead spikes during the time period of your effort.

- **Google Alerts**—Set alerts for your name, your company name, and keywords in your content. You'll get notified via an alert if your content or your message gets picked up and goes viral.

- **Back-Link Checkers**—Google Webmaster Tools enable you to check back-links going to your site during the same time period as your effort.

LINK POPULARITY CHECK

Link popularity analysis is one of the best ways to quantifiably and independently measure your website's online awareness. Some free web tools I use to check back-links are iwebtool.com and backlinkwatch.com.

Other free resources to check out include these:

www.seopro.com.au/free-seo-tools/link-checker/

www.iwebtool.com/backlink_checker

www.backlinkwatch.com/index.php

9

Monetize the Traffic: A Blueprint to Building a Site That Leverages SONAR

You've got the content. You've decided that the SONAR Content Distribution Model™ is the strategy for you. And you're now ready to jump in with both feet and start your SONAR marketing. Wait! Before you do so, you need to make sure your website is primed for the traffic and visibility it's going to be getting.

The next thing to do is evaluate and optimize your website to see if it has the elements and content needed for what I call the "SONAR 6":

1. **Sales**—Is your website positioned for cross-marketing, to entice visitor traffic with eye-catching banner ads linking to promotional pages? Do you have a storefront or a products page that is easily found off the main navigation bar?

2. **Lead generation**—Does your website have at least one mechanism (such as a sign-up box for a free newsletter or bonus report, or a link to a free product in exchange for filling out a questionnaire) to encourage visitors to give you their email addresses? Is this mechanism appealing and in a good location?

3. **Bonding**—Does your website have compelling, useful, and relevant content that will resonate with your target audience? Do you have a personal welcome message?

4. **Branding**—Does your website have a uniform message, logo, or tag line that is synonymous with your mission statement and business objective?

5. **SEO**—Has your site incorporated proper keyword tagging and other search engine techniques to help your web pages get indexed quickly and give it a better organic listing rank?

6. **Credibility**—Do you have information about yourself that highlights your education, accolades, milestones, and credentials? Does your site tell *your* story and focus on your unique selling proposition (USP)?

As you can see in Figure 9.1, this flow chart shows how the original (source) content is used, repurposed and distributed through each of the five SONAR platforms. These platforms trigger traffic and buzz about your website. Then, if your website is set up correctly to harness the traffic and buzz being created, it can also be leveraged and monetized for the SONAR 6: sales, lead generation, bonding, branding, SEO, and credibility.

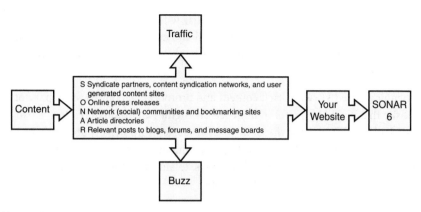

Figure 9.1   *The SONAR 6 process flow*

Dissecting the Ideal SONAR Website

Karen Keller, Ph.D., is a client and influence expert who specializes in female leadership and empowerment and who teaches the art of influence and persuasion for overall life success. Keller reached out to me in the middle of 2010 to help take her business to the next level—that is, she wanted to create and launch a redesigned website and free e-newsletter, as well as grow her subscriber base, increase website visibility and traffic, and extend her brand's reach.

Over the years, I've created, designed, and launched dozens of websites and newsletters. During this time, I have refined the entire creative sequence and launch strategy down to a science. Although every client's needs are different, most of the fundamental elements of success remain the same. Clients usually need a site with these characteristics:

- Visually appealing

- Friendly to both search engines and human readers

- Full of great content

- Poised to capture leads and sales

- Full of multimedia elements

- Reputable, establishing guru credibility and ability to promote branding

Because Keller already had great content from her existing blog, she was an ideal candidate for SONAR marketing and a SONAR-based website.

After chatting with Keller and getting familiar with her business model, target audience, and overall mission, I jumped right in and created her website wireframe—a blueprint, if you will, of the website's architecture, layout, color palette, features, and navigation.

I then developed keyword-rich content and promotional copy for each page of the website that would be useful to both search engines and human readers. I also added a few SEO tricks of the trade to increase keyword density and "link juice" (search engines favor relevant and high-ranking inter- and intrasite linking). Finally, I added several publishing elements, to aid in building Keller's subscriber list, promote sales, and bond with visitors.

 Note

Although I provide some tips throughout this book on optimizing your websites for search engines, this book isn't designed to be a guide to SEO. To learn more about SEO, I recommend that you pick up a copy of *The Truth About Search Engine Optimization*, by Rebecca Lieb, and *Outsmarting Google: SEO Secrets to Winning New Business*, by Evan Bailyn and Bradley Bailyn, both published by Pearson.

Although a good website is fluid and always changing based on user behavior patterns and business objectives, Figure 9.2 shows a "snapshot" of Keller's website after its October 2010 launch.

Now, I could have picked any one of the many websites I've worked on over the last decade or so to be an example of the "ideal" SONAR website. However, Keller's website is the most recent site that I launched from start to finish—specifically with the SONAR Content Distribution Model™ in mind. In addition, Keller's site is a textbook example of a complete SONAR website incorporating several SONAR 6 elements at once.

Many of the other sites I've worked on over the years have lost their full SONAR potency either because they changed their business objectives or had website revisions under new marketing direction. However, there are still some websites that I've either worked on or launched that continue to have some of the original SONAR elements I implemented. Those sites include JonnyBowden.com, TotalHealthBreakthroughs.com, EarlyToRise.com, and Bly.com—all of which I will discuss later in this chapter.

Because Keller's website snapshot is currently the most cohesive and comprehensive example of SONAR at this particular point in time, that's where I'd like to begin my focus.

As you can see in Figure 9.2, many elements and tools are used to harness the traffic created by SONAR. These SONAR 6 elements leverage sales, lead generation, bonding, branding, SEO, and credibility. Some of these specific tools include cross-selling banner ads, top placement logo for branding, three email collection boxes for lead generation efforts, testimonials for credibility, keyword cloud for SEO, and sample newsletter issues/articles for bonding.

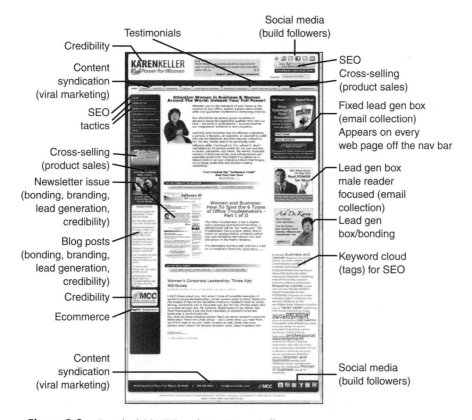

Figure 9.2 *An ideal SONAR website: Karen-Keller.com*

Lead Generation

The basis for any publishing site is content, so the goal is to use your content to gain relevant email addresses and build your subscriber database (lead generation). You can go about this in several ways.

The most common is to have an e-newsletter sign-up box on the home page (see Figure 9.3). This should be a fixed (static) location that appears on every page of your website; you never know what the port of entry will be to organic visitors (meaning you won't know exactly how visitors arrive on any given page). They might come in through one of your subpages that appears in the organic search results, not necessarily through your home page. The e-news box should be above the fold—ideally, in the upper-right corner, based on eye-tracking studies. It should have a strong headline and offer an incentive, such as a free subscription, a free bonus report, or both. The e-news box should also be eye-catching. Another industry standard is to have your privacy policy near your Click Here Now button, to assure visitors that your intentions are honorable.

Because you never know what will strike a reader's fancy, I like to test a few different lead-generation elements on a home page to see which one works best with website visitors. In addition to the sign-up box, I like try relevant public opinion polls and targeted banner ads with a specific call to action (see Figures 9.4, 9.5, and 9.6).

When using lead-generation elements, in which visitors are required to give their email address, I include a disclosure statement about email use, as well as a link to the privacy policy. Following is a sample disclaimer:

> Email address is required for order confirmation notice, as well as to receive special messages from Dr. Keller. In addition, as a free gift, all customers receive a courtesy subscription to Dr. Keller's acclaimed free newsletter, *Influence It! Real Power for Women*, which they can opt out of at any time.

Now, because the primary audience for this site is women, a special banner ad is in place as not to turn away any potential customers or subscribers who aren't women (see Figure 9.4). This targeted ad is a great way to grab the attention of male visitors who arrive at the website, letting them know services are applicable to them as well. The special ad then redirects to a landing page with a relevant message just for that audience. In addition, there's another banner ad that encourages website visitors to engage with Keller (a clinical psychologist and Master Certified Coach with more than 25 years of experience) and pick her brain on virtually any life question, aptly titled "Ask Dr. Karen" (see Figure 9.6). A tool like this is good for bonding, branding, and prospecting.

Another way to build your email database is to add an opt-in and disclosure statement on your purchase order form. Not every visitor will sign up for your e-newsletter or take your poll. Many visitors might know exactly what they want and go straight for the purchase. In those scenarios, you can give all paying customers a complementary subscription to your free e-newsletter—just clearly disclose that you're doing so.

On or before your order form, where a customer enters contact information, and near the field for email address, add the following verbiage:

> *Note:* You are about to enter a secure area to begin the order process. Any data you submit to us through an online order form is transferred to us via Secure Sockets Layer, an encryption protocol, and is kept in data-bases that cannot be accessed from outside our firewall. When entering your contact information on our order form, your email address will be required so that we can send your order confirmation notice, as well as send you special messages from Dr. Keller. In addition, all customers will receive a special, complementary subscription to Dr. Keller's acclaimed free newsletter, *Influence It! Real Power for Women*, which they can opt out of at any time. Your email address will never be rented or sold to any third party. To view our complete privacy policy, _click here_.

By doing this, you're following good email practices and also increasing the reach of your publication. You're also offering something for free, which all consumers like.

As you can see from Figure 9.3, the e-news sign-up box has a compelling headline geared toward the target reader as well as focuses on main primary free incentive: the bonus report. For added value, the reader is offered a secondary incentive, a complimentary subscription to the weekly e-newsletter. To alleviate any concerns about spam, there is a link to a Privacy Policy. And a visual element of the free report is added to help make the report more tangible.

Figure 9.3   *E-news sign-up: Karen-Keller.com*

Because the overall website is geared toward women, the banner ad shown in Figure 9.4 was added and is aimed at male visitors. This secondary element is a good way to remain focused on your primary target audience as well as open opportunities for other demographics. Since the foundational message of the website is appealing to both sexes, this tactic was ideal. As far as aesthetics are concerned, the banner ad matches the page's color palette but also speaks to the target reader with a captivating headline. There are actually two banner ads that rotate randomly in this space. So the messages are cohesive, yet different. This is done with the idea that if one message doesn't appeal to a reader, a second message that appears on a return visit will resonate with the visitor.

Figure 9.4   *Male-focused banner ad: Karen-Keller.com*

Adding a poll element is a good ad-hoc banner to test between other advertising messages. As you can see in Figure 9.5, the tactic here is to engage the reader with a notable personality or message that is appealing and encourages website interaction. As with most of the lead-generation efforts, poll takers receive fully disclosed bonuses for their participation (free bonus report and free subscription to e-newsletter).

Figure 9.5   *Public opinion poll banner ad: Karen-Keller.com*

Another powerful tool for both lead generation and bonding purposes is allowing the reader to ask questions to the website's main expert. As you can see in Figure 9.6, this is done via an "Ask Dr. Karen" banner ad, in which website visitors can ask virtually any question in exchange for their email addresses. Again, it is fully disclosed that visitors submitting questions are automatically signed up for the free e-newsletter, which they can opt out of at any time.

Figure 9.6 *Ask Dr. Karen advice tool (home page banner ad): Karen-Keller.com*

After a male visitor clicks the banner ad shown earlier in Figure 9.4, he is redirected to a landing page. As you can see from Figure 9.7, this page is written specifically with men in mind, addressing most of the circumstances that they would seek out the expert's services for—in other words—problem vs. solution. The free e-newsletter and bonus report are also featured on the landing page for extra incentive.

Figure 9.7 *Male-focused landing page: Karen-Keller.com*

After a poll taker clicks the banner ad referred to in Figure 9.5, she is redirected to a landing page where she can take a short poll and have the opportunity to share her thoughts about the topic in question (see Figure 9.8). In general, your poll questions should be something that your target audience will find interesting. You want your audience to be able to relate to the questions you're asking. As with the other lead-generation elements, full disclosure is given about poll participation and complimentary e-newsletter sign up. In addition, the anti-spam and Privacy Policy is mentioned. Lastly, visitors are advised that results from the poll may be shared with media outlets and published in the e-newsletter or on the website.

Figure 9.8   *Public opinion poll page: Karen-Keller.com*[1]

Website visitors who click on the "Ask Dr. Karen" banner shown in Figure 9.6 are redirected to the online form to submit a question to the expert (see Figure 9.9). The form page is simple with only a few fields for the visitor to provide basic information and ask a question. As with the other online elements, this form also has the disclosure that users will be automatically signed up for a complimentary e-newsletter subscription, from which they can unsubscribe at any time.

1. Public opinion poll page: Karen-Keller.com. Poll images were selected from public domain locations or free stock photography: http://en.wikipedia.org/wiki/File:Hillary_Clinton_official_Secretary_of_State_portrait_crop.jpg and http://www.acclaimimages.com/_gallery/_pages/0519-0910-2111-1545.html.

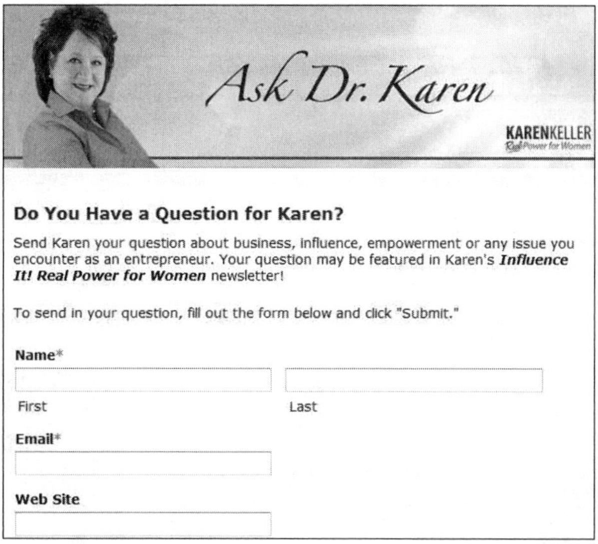
Ask Dr. Karen

KARENKELLER

Do You Have a Question for Karen?

Send Karen your question about business, influence, empowerment or any issue you encounter as an entrepreneur. Your question may be featured in Karen's ***Influence It! Real Power for Women*** newsletter!

To send in your question, fill out the form below and click "Submit."

Name*

First Last

Email*

Web Site

Figure 9.9 *Ask Dr. Karen advice tool (landing page): Karen-Keller.com*

As you can see in Figure 9.10, the website has embraced social media marketing by incorporating icons for some of the most popular social media networks on the Web—all of which hyperlink to the expert's profile pages on each respective social media page. These icons are located in prime real estate on the home page: top-right corner. This social media connection helps promote congruity between the expert and their visitors, so users can actively engage with the expert on their social media platform of choice whenever they like.

Links to social media

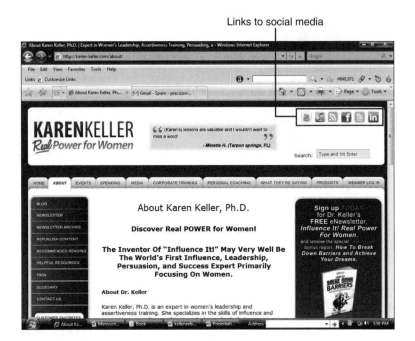

Figure 9.10   *Lead generation via social media: Karen-Keller.com*

Sales and Cross-Selling

Whether you're selling a product, a service or both, having an easy-to-find, eye-catching mechanism that helps monetize your SONAR website traffic is essential to your bottom line. This can be accomplished through your navigation bar (nav bar) and website ads.

The ideal location on your nav bar is top center/right. Eye-tracking studies have shown that this is where eyes gravitate first. Your nav bar title should be noticeable and easy to read. It should also be simple. Classic titles for nav bar e-commerce include these:

- Store
- Shop
- Products
- Products & Services
- Shop now!
- Online store
- Store

...having an easy-to-find, eyecatching mechanism that helps monetize your SONAR website traffic is essential to your bottom line.

The general idea is to make this page easy to find for the people visiting your website. You don't want to have to make visitors figure out where your products are located within your website; the location should be clear and obvious.

Ads—banner or text—should also be attention-grabbing and in prime locations. Ideal placement for a banner ad is either near content or above the fold (the top half of the web page). If an ad is below the fold, make sure it's appealing—either with a strong headline or a striking visual image.

With banner ads, the unit size might vary depending on your website framework. Typical sizes include medium rectangles (300×250), small squares (125×125), rectangles (180×150), and leaderboards (728×90).

 Note

> For a complete list of Internet marketing unit (IMU) sizes, visit the Internet Advertising Bureau (IAB) at www.iab.net/iab_products_and_industry_services/1421/1443/1452.

Studies have shown that you have about three seconds to grab someone's attention, so a compelling headline and strong visual image are critical for a good click-through rate.

To avoid inundation of banner ads and overwhelming website visitors, it's a good idea to have a small amount of fixed banner ad locations. You can then have ads rotate in those locations either at timed intervals or each time the page is refreshed. For example, you might have three banner ad spots, but each banner ad can rotate with up to three messages each. So, it's like having nine messages without taking up too much banner ad space. Because each ad can be programmed to serve images randomly with even exposures, this is a great way to test different approaches with copywriting or graphic design.

The ads should then link to a dedicated promotional landing page, not a catalog page with many different products. Instead, the ads should link to a specific page that relates to the banner ad. This helps keep clarity of vision and streamlines the path the customer should take to purchase a specific item.

I recommend also having a banner ad on the website under a Customer Favorites title (see Figure 9.11). Consumer studies have shown that people are influenced by what other consumers buy (the most popular items, favorites) and reviews. It's psychological purchase behavior. Did you ever click an item of interest, and then a related item appears on the side of the web page asking you, "If you like this, you may like this too." These are all popular etailing tactics with well-known websites such as Amazon.com, Blockbuster.com, BabiesRUs.com, JCPenney.com, and more.

Also, to help alleviate consumer concerns about online purchasing, it's a good idea to display any logos from merchant accounts and Secure Socket Layer (SSL) certificates such as PayPal or VeriSign (see Figure 9.12). If you're a member of the Better Business Bureau, incorporate this banner or logo on your home page and product page as well.

On pages with content that appears more informational in nature, it's important to have a clear and direct call to action on the page, telling the consumer what to do next: click a link, call an 800-number, send an email, and so on.

This gives visitors to your website some direction—you're helping steer them into your sales funnel by encouraging their next move toward customer or client.

As you can see from Figure 9.11, a fixed banner ad was added to the home page, above the fold (top portion of the web page), so that it's viewable on every page of the website. These means that no matter which page organic traffic may take a visitor to on the website, there's a promotional element touting a "customer favorite" product.

Figure 9.11   *Cross-selling banner ad: Karen-Keller.com*

Many website users are unsure about the privacy and security about online purchasing. To help alleviate this, it's a best practice to let visitors know on your website that you have secure ordering and use a reputable online merchant. As you can see from Figure 9.12, securing ordering through well-known ecommerce platform, PayPal, is mentioned.

In addition to individual banner ads promoting particular products, it's important to have your online store or ecommerce section easily found by website visitors. As you can see in Figure 9.13, this is typically accomplished by using the top navigation bar, and titling one of the tabs or links as "Products." Other popular titles include "Online Store," "Shop," "Store," or "Catalog." You don't want to use titles that are easily overlooked by consumers. Familiarity is best. You want location and title to simplify the user experience and take the buyer to the product as quick as possible.

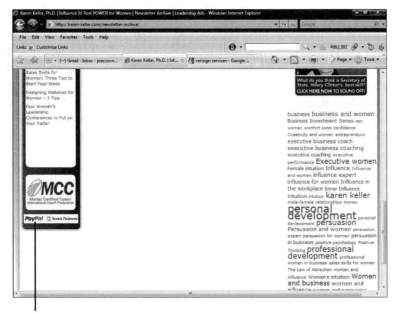

If you accept PayPal,
be sure to say so!

Figure 9.12 *PayPal logo for e-commerce: Karen-Keller.com*

Make your online store easy to find

Figure 9.13 *Cross-selling products page: Karen-Keller.com*

As you see in Figure 9.14, the Products page is virtually a catalog webpage of the various products and services offered. There is standard introduction copy prefacing the purpose of the online store to website visitors. This also includes solicitation copy asking visitors for feedback on potential products they'd like to see offered. This is a great way to instill a customer-centric philosophy and create products based on actual customer demand. There's also several product boxes on the page, each containing the product name, type of product (that is, ebook and so on), product image (which when clicked takes the reader to an enlarged photo), a description, and price.

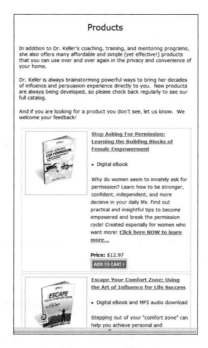

Figure 9.14 *Cross-selling products—catalog page: Karen-Keller.com*

On most every page of your website, it's important to have a call to action. A call to action simply tells the reader what he should do next. The idea is to make this next step obvious and straightforward. As you can see in Figure 9.15, the last paragraph on the personal coaching page, the call to action alerts the reader that they can schedule a free 15-minute consultation with the expert to see if coaching services may be right for them. Then there's a clickable hyperlink that enables a new email with the experts email address and subject line already pre-populated, so all the consumer has to do is enter his contact information and hit sent.

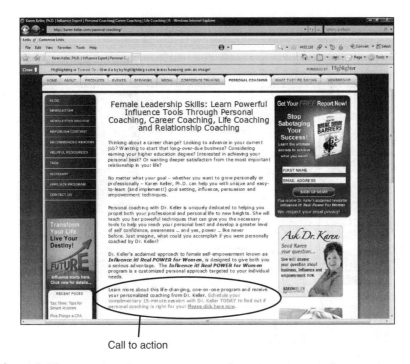

Call to action

Figure 9.15   *Sample call to action—personal coaching: Karen-Keller.com*

As you can see in Figure 9.16, the last paragraph on the corporate training, the call to action is asking the reader if she wants to schedule a complementary session to determine if corporate training is right for her. But before they do so, they must click to answer a few short questions. Having a short online survey is a great way to qualify prospects to see if the potential relationship is mutually beneficial.

Call to action

Figure 9.16 *Sample call to action—corporate training web page: Karen-Keller.com*

As you can see in Figure 9.17, the last paragraph on the professional speaking page, the call to action is simple: Contact the expert for your specific needs. The email address is also clickable, so clicking it automatically launches a new email window that is pre-populated to be sent to the email address mentioned. All the reader has to do is type in his or her needs and contact info.

Call to action

Figure 9.17   *Sample call to action—speaking web page: Karen-Keller.com*

Boosting Your E-Commerce Sales

In a tough economic environment, both retail and e-tail sales can be hard to achieve. But a few simple yet powerful tips can help you boost online sales and gain loyal customers:[2]

1. **Display your SSL seal prominently**—Secure Socket Layer (SSL) is a sign that the site is encrypted, meaning that the information your consumers enter—such as personal and credit card information—is protected. Most e-commerce sites must file for an SSL certificate from vendors such as VeriSign, GoDaddy, eTrust, or TRUSTe. If you're using PayPal, display its logo showing secure payments. It's a good practice to display these images on your order page, as well as make sure that the "https" or image of a lock is present in the browser window. This is a clear and comforting sign to consumers that they can order online with confidence.

---

2. Source: http://musclemarketing.blogspot.com/2009/08/boost-your-ecommerce-sales.html.

2. **Encourage online sales in place of other order mechanisms**—Offer special "Internet-only pricing" to customers, perhaps at a discount of 5% to 10%. This reduces potential overhead costs for staffing fees, such as telesales or order-entry personnel.

3. **Offer free shipping**—Many e-tailers already factor shipping into their published price, so when there's a big, flashing banner next to the item saying "Free Shipping," it gives consumers that extra push to move forward with the transaction. It boils down to basic psychology. Everyone likes to feel that they're getting something for free.

4. **Use buyer feedback to your advantage—Create a Customer Favorites or Hot Item button** on your website. Also include glowing customer testimonials (when you get them) next to the product for potential prospects to see. Consumers like to feel good about the item they're about to purchase. Seeing a great testimonial and knowing that others have been happy with their purchase provides validation for the purchase. In addition to helping with the conversion, this tactic reduces buyer remorse and product returns.

5. **Advertise products in Google Product Search (formerly Froogle)**— At the time of this writing, Google Product Search was in beta form, but still worth checking out. This is a free product information platform from Google that allows you to post (upload) a single item or submit a tab-delimited data feed (via a spreadsheet program such as .txt or .xls). This is ideal for multiple product entries or a list of products. Your products will appear in Google Product Search and may also appear in Google.com search results, depending on the keywords used.

 Note

For more information on how to set up a Google Product Search or data feed, visit www.google.com/intl/en_us/products/submit.html or www.google.com/support/merchants/bin/answer.py?answer=160588.

6. **Make sure your product pages are optimized for search engines**— After doing some keyword research on actual search behavior for your product, refine your meta description, your meta keywords, and the title tag of your product pages. This helps consumers find your product in the organic listing of search engine results.

7. **Place a special coupon code banner on your home page**—This is a best practice with online fashion retailers. There's typically a banner ad on the home page stating something like, "Summer Blowout Sale, Use

Coupon Code 1234." This is another great way to offer a special discount for your online customers that makes them feel good about the purchase. You can encourage viral activity by having a Forward to Friend text link that opens an new email window with the coupon or coupon code. Be sure to have some great intro copy mentioning that customers should "pass on the great savings to friends, family, and colleagues."

8. **Consider payment plans**—For your bigger-ticket items, consider setting up extended payment plans that allow customers to pay for an item over a few payments. If an item costs $200, you might want to offer a flex pay of "6 easy payments of $33.33" that is conveniently autobilled to the purchaser's credit card. Just be diligent when calculating your payment prices and creating your return/refund policy for these items. The general rule is to cover your actual production costs/hard costs in the first one to three payments.

 Note

Remember to continue testing various ways of improving sales and driving prospects to your storefront. Make note of when you implement new tactics, such as the ones I describe in this section. After a month of each tactic being live, compare sales results year-over-year to see if you've found the sweet spot in your e-commerce efforts. I'm confident that you will see an improvement in online sales.

Bonding

Your website is your tool for speaking to visitors and subscribers. Your goal is to build and cultivate a relationship that takes the visitor from stranger to friend. Next, you want to move this friend across the sales funnel to customer, multi-buyer, and advocate.

> Your goal is to build and cultivate a relationship that takes the visitor from stranger to friend.

This doesn't happen overnight. It requires strong, captivating, and compelling editorial that is relevant to your readers' interests and offers them something of value. It also requires the guru to be transparent—to be him- or herself and speak directly to the reader. You'll get loyal readers who buy into your message and mission. Ultimately, these are the people you want on your list.

Your site should also highlight your experience. After all, people want to follow someone who's an expert in a certain field—someone they can learn from. That's why it's essential to have pages on your website that highlight personal and professional milestones, academic achievements, media appearances, honors and awards, and any other noteworthy accolades that shines the light on your expertise and credibility.

I also advise clients to add a personal message that tells the unique story of who they are and how they landed where they are today. This not only adds authenticity to the site, but it also lets readers know you're a real person who can relate to their needs.

As you can see from Figure 9.18, you can speak to your website visitors directly through carefully crafted home page copy as well as having a welcome message (which evokes that warm, fuzzy feeling), an "About" or "Bio" page (highlighting expert's credentials, experience, accolades, and so on), and reader testimonials or feedback. The later is a great way for visitors to see real-life examples of how other subscribers or customers are relating with the expert. Before you publish any testimonials on your website, make sure you have prior authorization from the person who issued the testimonial as well as find out how they'd like to be mentioned albeit full name, first name and last initial, just initials as well as state of residence. Testimonials give a refreshing third-party perspective to prospects as well as reinforces expert's appeal to existing customers. .

Figure 9.18 *Bonding through a welcome message, testimonials, and more:* Karen-Keller.com

Search Engine Optimization (SEO)

If I had a dollar for every time I said the following to potential clients, I'd be rich: "A website's no good if no one can find it."

Many clients come to me saying that they don't have money for SEO. Or they don't have time for SEO. Or they don't think SEO is important.

They don't realize that writing for search engines is just as important as writing for human reader—your website visitors and subscribers.

When building or revamping your website, it's important to get a good SEO specialist on board, to ensure that you have the proper keywords, tagging, and density for each page.

If you're a do-it-yourselfer, follow the basic keyword research steps in Chapter 2, "Online Content Syndication: What You Need to Know," using Google Keyword External Tool and similar free online tools. Most importantly, before you start your research, you must define your 10–15 root keywords. These are your primary keywords that encompass your website, your message, your target audience, and your unique selling proposition (USP).

After defining your root keywords, you use the aforementioned tools to view search popularity and variations of your root keywords. You then use those primary keywords and variations in your title tags, meta description, meta keywords, and alt tags, as well as in your actual body text.

You can incorporate other tricks on your website to aid your SEO efforts, as follows:

- **FAQs**—A frequently asked questions (FAQ) or Q&A page is a great way to address typical real-life questions that your website visitors want to know about. This is great for bonding and subscriber relations. It's also good for SEO because it's a means of adding keyword-rich sentences to your website. For best results with readers and search engines, make content on this page unique, fresh, and creative. For authenticity, don't copy and paste it from elsewhere on the Web (see Figure 9.19).

- **Resource page**—A resource page is another way to provide useful information to readers, such as relevant websites, books, or other sources of interest. However, with the right resources, it's also a place that can be keyword rich. In addition, this is an ideal location for relevant link building (through link exchanges, reciprocal link programs, and back-linking) or affiliate marketing opportunities. When you find synergistic websites or partners, you can offer them a link exchange: You place a small descriptive text or banner ad about their website and a link to their site on your resource page. Your partner then recipro- cates on with a description and link back to your site. You can also put synergistic affiliate banner ads here. Traffic to this page could turn into sales splits, which can be an ancillary revenue stream for your business (see Figure 9.20).

- **Glossary**—A Glossary page might not be applicable for every website, but my view is that it's better to give more information than less. All industries have some nomenclatures or terms that can be defined for the average person. This makes your website user-friendly and provides another way to work those primary keywords into your body content. The important point to remember here is that glossary terms need to be unique and relevant to the website. You won't get the full SEO bene- fit if you simply copy and paste a glossary that's already on the Web. This involves a balance of SEO, creativity, and technical writing experi- ence (see Figure 9.21).

- **Keyword cloud**—Incorporating a keyword cloud is a great way to show site visitors your target words. This reinforces to visitors and subscribers that your site meets their editorial (content) needs. It also helps with SEO because the keywords are part of the page's body con- tent. Keyword clouds can typically be used with content-management plug-ins such as WordPress (see Figure 9.22).

 Note

A keyword cloud is simply a text box somewhere on your website (usually lower, right portion), that is filled with your keywords. Typically, this is enabled with WordPress-based websites.

- **Newsletter archives**—Search engines like categorization. And, of course, I've already stressed incorporating keywords into your body content is important. Setting up your newsletter archives correctly is user-friendly because it helps visitors easily find back issues and content at a glance. Proper archiving also helps with your SEO efforts (see Figure 9.23).

For instance, by sorting your issues by category, you are using your root keywords and also identifying relevant topics to help your visitors easily find articles of interest. In addition, sorting by date helps readers find recent issues if they don't know the topic. Drilling down further, segmenting content by author is another great way to be user-friendly and tap into some of your well-known editorial contributors who have a strong web presence.

Frequently asked questions or Q&A pages can be informative and educational for the reader, but also have an added value to search engines. As you can see in Figure 9.19, questions can be relevant and useful while allowing you to weave in select targeted keywords. These can be general questions, industry related questions, or operational questions. When you sit down to write these, try to put yourself in the shoes of the reader. What would they really like to know? What information would benefit them? Then, after you write your questions and answers organically, pepper in keywords where applicable.

Figure 9.19   *Sample FAQs page: Karen-Keller.com*

As you can see in Figure 9.20, a resource page is an ideal location to put back-links to relevant websites either through affiliate marketing, joint ventures, cross-promotional or link exchange efforts. You can start your page with synergistic links, for reader reference purposes, then build your page from there to include text links or banner ads that aid in sales growth. For either reason, the relevancy between back-links helps with your SEO efforts.

Figure 9.20   *Sample resource page: Karen-Keller.com*

As you can see from Figure 9.21, a glossary page is another tool that can be both advantageous to website visitors (human readers) as well as search engines. The goal is to write unique, relevant, useful, and keyword-rich definitions that add value to the website as well as aid in SEO efforts.

As you can see from Figure 9.22, a keyword cloud is a section on the home page of a website that pulls in relevant keywords that are used on the website. This complements your SEO efforts and is easily implementable with use of a search engine-friendly content management system, such as WordPress. Typically, these are clickable "tags" that link to related content (articles) within the website.

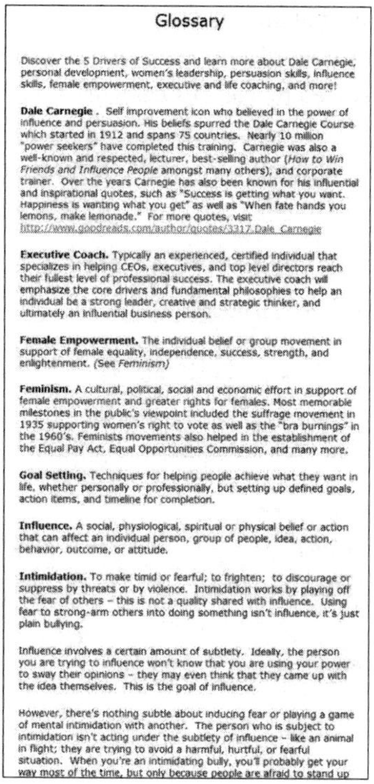

Glossary

Discover the 5 Drivers of Success and learn more about Dale Carnegie, personal development, women's leadership, persuasion skills, influence skills, female empowerment, executive and life coaching, and more!

Dale Carnegie . Self improvement icon who believed in the power of influence and persuasion. His beliefs spurred the Dale Carnegie Course which started in 1912 and spans 75 countries. Nearly 10 million "power seekers" have completed this training. Carnegie was also a well-known and respected, lecturer, best-selling author (*How to Win Friends and Influence People* amongst many others), and corporate trainer. Over the years Carnegie has also been known for his influential and inspirational quotes, such as "Success is getting what you want. Happiness is wanting what you get" as well as "When fate hands you lemons, make lemonade." For more quotes, visit http://www.goodreads.com/author/quotes/3317.Dale_Carnegie

Executive Coach. Typically an experienced, certified individual that specializes in helping CEOs, executives, and top level directors reach their fullest level of professional success. The executive coach will emphasize the core drivers and fundamental philosophies to help an individual be a strong leader, creative and strategic thinker, and ultimately an influential business person.

Female Empowerment. The individual belief or group movement in support of female equality, independence, success, strength, and enlightenment. *(See Feminism)*

Feminism. A cultural, political, social and economic effort in support of female empowerment and greater rights for females. Most memorable milestones in the public's viewpoint included the suffrage movement in 1935 supporting women's right to vote as well as the "bra burnings" in the 1960's. Feminists movements also helped in the establishment of the Equal Pay Act, Equal Opportunities Commission, and many more.

Goal Setting. Techniques for helping people achieve what they want in life, whether personally or professionally, but setting up defined goals, action items, and timeline for completion.

Influence. A social, physiological, spiritual or physical belief or action that can affect an individual person, group of people, idea, action, behavior, outcome, or attitude.

Intimidation. To make timid or fearful; to frighten; to discourage or suppress by threats or by violence. Intimidation works by playing off the fear of others – this is not a quality shared with influence. Using fear to strong-arm others into doing something isn't influence, it's just plain bullying.

Influence involves a certain amount of subtlety. Ideally, the person you are trying to influence won't know that you are using your power to sway their opinions – they may even think that they came up with the idea themselves. This is the goal of influence.

However, there's nothing subtle about inducing fear or playing a game of mental intimidation with another. The person who is subject to intimidation isn't acting under the subtlety of influence – like an animal in flight; they are trying to avoid a harmful, hurtful, or fearful situation. When you're an intimidating bully, you'll probably get your way most of the time, but only because people are afraid to stand up

Figure 9.21 *Sample glossary page: Karen-Keller.com*

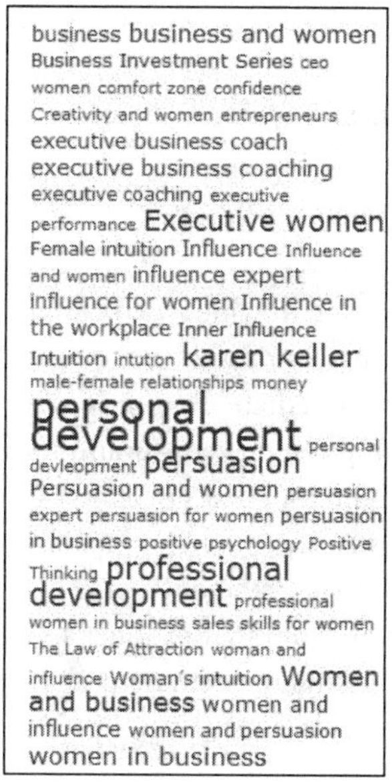

Figure 9.22 *Keyword cloud: Karen-Keller.com*

Search engines favor pages that are easy to index. This includes pages that have information in groups or categories. As you can see from Figure 9.23, a newsletter archive that has content sorted by various categories such as topic, month, or publication is not only attractive to search engines, but also user-friendly to website readers as well helping them obtain editorial information quickly and with ease.

Figure 9.23   *Categorized newsletter archives: Karen-Keller.com*

Branding

Branding is a form of marketing in which a consumer sees or hears an advertisers message (via email, TV, print ad, or radio spot), but doesn't necessarily respond right away. The action isn't immediate. Branding is hard to measure and hard to quantify. Typically, it's assumption driven—brand marketers often tie campaigns or events into a timeline and look for spikes in traffic or sales to see if there's correlation with the branding efforts. The marketer has to hope that once the consumer sees/hears the message, he or she remembers it. The ultimate goal is that consumer has enough name recognition from that product so he or she isn't distracted by competitive brands when making the actual purchase.

Note

Advertising studies show that the average consumer needs to see a message 7–8 times before it becomes familiar to him or her.

This contrasts with direct response marketing, in which there is generally one strong message with a compelling offer. This message can come via an email, newsletter ad, direct letter, or an online ad but has typically one main call to action, such as "Click here now." The major difference between direct response marketing and branding: In direct response marketing, your results are immediate and quantifiable.

Branding efforts take time because you must develop your brand loyalty with your target audience first, to help overall conversions. Think of some well-known products and their recognizable brands, such as McDonald's and its Golden Arches; Nike and its popular swoosh image; or BMW and its slogan, "The Ultimate Driving Machine," and trademark black, white, and blue propeller-inspired logo. These companies spend hundreds of millions of dollars on brand development to make their image, logo, slogan, or tag line instantly recognizable by consumers.

And it works.

Quick story: The other day, I was driving past McDonald's with my son, who's nearly three years old. He looked out the window and said, "Mama, I'm hungry— Happy Meal." Now, my son is smart, but by no means can he read yet. He can't read the word *McDonald's*, but he did see the infamous Golden Arches and associated that immediately with a Happy Meal I had bought him before. Another time, we were at the supermarket in line, and the woman in front of us had a six-pack of Coca-Cola. My son looked and said, "Coca-Cola." I know he didn't read the red-and-white script, but he did recognize the font style Coke uses and immediately associated it with the product.

As a marketer, business owner, or entrepreneur, your job is to incorporate your brand, image, slogan, tag line, or logo into your website. You want your message to be clear, prevalent, cohesive, and consistent. Your brand should be the same across all platforms—Web, stationery, fulfillment, products, and promotional material.

Your brand should be the same across all platforms—Web, stationery, fulfillment, products, and promotional material.

As you can see from Figure 9.24, it's important for brand cohesiveness and congruity for any logo, tag line, or slogan to be in a prominent, fixed location on the website. Typically, this is in the masthead or "leader board" area (top of page) of the website so it appears on any every page no matter where a visitor may be. This helps with brand recognition and awareness.

Figure 9.24   *Brand integration: Karen-Keller.com*

In addition to logos, tag lines, and slogans, there's other branding elements that are part of your business. For example, as you can see in Figure 9.25, having a thumbnail image of the newsletter not only helps with bonding, but promotes the newsletter as its own brand—the look, feel, fonts, and so on. The thumbnail can be clickable and hyperlink to the most recent newsletter issue as an extra value-added bonus, giving prospects a sample of what they would receive if they signed up.

Thumbnails are a nice touch

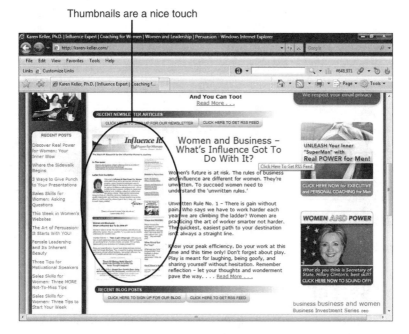

Figure 9.25   *Brand integration: Karen-Keller.com*

Credibility

Being an expert in your field is extremely important, whether you're a speaker, a newsletter publisher, or a consultant. People like to follow someone who knows more than them, a specialist at what they do—a "guru," if you will.

But you also need the credentials to back up your expertise. That's why I tell clients to not only create a personal welcome message on their website home page that speaks to the consumer, but also have an About or Bio page on the website that showcases their milestones, accomplishments, accolades, professional awards, affiliations, memberships, and educational achievements (see Figure 9.26).

This helps cement your expert status and highlights your personal and professional accomplishments. It clearly shows why you are the person they need to listen to in order to help them achieve their goals.

Figure 9.26   *Credibility and personal message: Karen-Keller.com*

More "Best of" SONAR Websites...

As I mentioned earlier in this chapter, I've worked on many websites over the years for respected and well-known publishers. As time goes by, these sites have undergone changes from my original blueprint either due a new business model or new marketing direction.

However, some of these websites such as JonnyBowden.com, EarlyToRise.com, TotalHealthBreakthroughs.com, and Bly.com still display some of my SONAR elements as well as other popular tactics that complement SONAR 6. I'd like to review these sites now.

As you can see in Figure 9.27, an interstitial on your home page is a great way to introduce a new product or special offer. In this case, Early To Rise (ETR) is using it for lead-generation purposes touting their free e-newsletter subscription, as well as special free "in-depth" report from wealth-building guru, Michael Masterson. This is a popular tactic to keep visitors focused on a special offer, but is not the same as the dreaded pop-up ad (which can be blocked by some websites and computer settings). Having the main website in the backdrop and the call to action center stage easily keeps the reader's eyes on the main message, all the while an obvious 'X' is apparent to close the interstitial, if the reader is not interested.

Figure 9.27 *Using interstitials to get a reader's attention: EarlyToRise.com*

A great way to encourage website visitors to republish (syndicate) your content for free and create viral marketing is to simply tell them to do so. This is an element I added to most every content-based website I worked on over the past decade to help aid in SONAR marketing efforts, especially sites I launched including Total Health Breakthroughs (THB). As you can see in Figure 9.28, on the bottom part of their home page, THB has a call out to "Editors, Publishers, Marketers, Bloggers, and Webmasters" advising that their content is ripe for the pickins'. All that needs to be done is simply adding THB's attribution statement and back-link in the republished content, thereby sourcing the original content and helps with branding, visibility, SEO, and traffic generation.

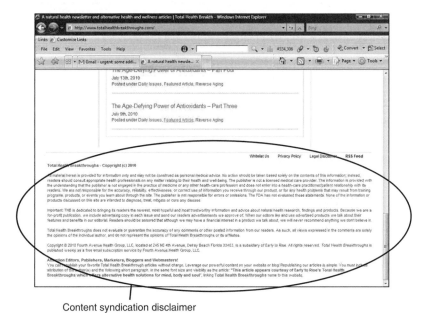

Content syndication disclaimer

Figure 9.28 *Content syndication disclaimers help with viral marketing: TotalHealthBreakthroughs.com*

Because many of Dr. Jonny Bowden's readers may also find his content interesting to republish, I added a similar syndication element to Jonny's website which asks the reader, "Like what you've read...republish it!" As you can see in Figure 9.29, Jonny has a similar statement for author attribution as well as back-link to his site to help with branding, visibility, SEO, and traffic generation.

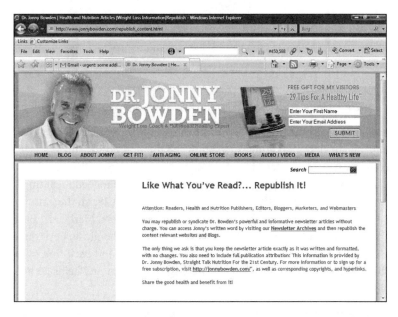

Figure 9.29 *Content syndication disclaimers also helps with branding, market visibility, SEO, and traffic generation: JonnyBowden.com*

As mentioned earlier in the book, one of the best locations as far as eye tracking is the top right of a webpage. To this end, when I launched TotalHealthBreakthroughs.com, I wanted the sign-up box in prime real estate to capture organic website visits as well as stand out. As you can see in Figure 9.30, the sign-up box is in the ideal location on the home page. It also is short and to the point, having a strong call to action (sign up now!) and citing the value proposition (free health newsletter). Also a best practice, I included a link to the Privacy Policy, so visitors can see that their email addresses aren't being exploited.

Privacy statement   Easy to find sign up

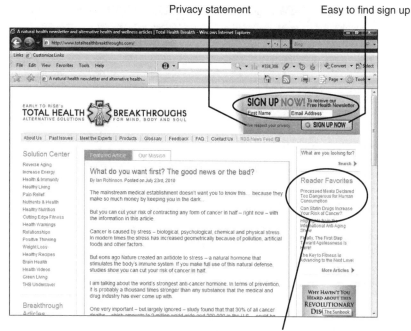

Figure 9.30   *Reader's Favorites helps with bonding: TotalHealthBreakthroughs.com*

It's human nature to have interest in other's behavior...what they are doing, reading, buying, and more. To this avail, letting website visitors know what other visitors are reading is something that actually helps bonding efforts but also is a value-added service showing which articles are the most popular. As you saw in Figure 9.30, I tapped into this psychological curiosity and incorporated a Reader's Favorites element when I launched THB.com. This section has the most popular article titles and redirects to the entire article.

There are many ways you can use content to help with SEO efforts. As you can see in Figures 9.31 and 9.32, a few of the most effective ways are to create original, value-oriented, keyword-dense web pages that include definitions (Glossary) and frequency asked questions (FAQs). These types of web pages should be targeted to your ideal prospect and contain useful information. I wrote the THB Glossary and FAQ pages to ensure that the site got the full SEO benefit (original content) but also wrote the pages through the eyes of the ideal THB subscriber—what would they likely want to know?

Figure 9.31 *Keyword-rich, reader-friendly pages, such as this Glossary, help with SEO and add value: TotalHealthBreakthroughs.com*

Figure 9.32 *Keyword-rich, reader-friendly pages, such as this FAQ, help with SEO and add value: TotalHealthBreakthroughs.com*

A popular SEO tactic is to list archived content into groupings such as issue, date, topic, and author. This categorization not only helps search engines index the page faster, but it also has reader value: it saves time and is extremely subscriber-centric. As you can see in Figure 9.33, I implemented this tactic on both THB and Jonny Bowden websites and it makes finding back issues much easier.

Figure 9.33 *Archiving your content into groups is both reader friendly and search engine friendly: TotalHealthBreakthroughs.com and JonnyBowden.com*

In addition to having lead-generation elements on your home page to help list-building efforts, it's important to have sales elements for immediate monetization. These elements typically take the form of banner ads. As you can see in Figure 9.34, when I launched THB, I designated a prime location at the fold (mid-point of page) and near the content that would house a few small square banner ads. The product ads are synergistic to editorial content and redirect to info products (paid ebooks).

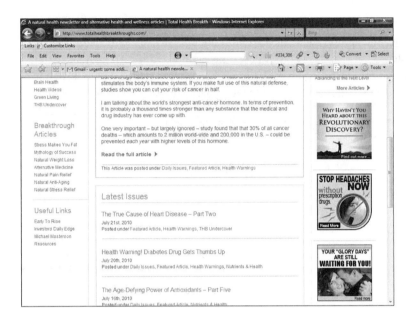

Figure 9.34 *Converting your website traffic into sales helps monetize SONAR and other online marketing efforts: TotalHealthBreakthroughs.com*

It's always good to offer more than one lead-generation (email sign-up) element on your website. In the event that one doesn't catch a reader's fancy, the other might. It's also good to encourage social media interaction by linking back to your social media profile pages. As you can see in Figure 9.35, there are a few value-added freebies: DM ROI Calculator, B2B marketing handbook, and e-newsletter. Also, in close proximity to the special free offers are recognizable icons to Facebook, Twitter, and LinkedIn to encourage social interaction with the publisher.

> It's always good to offer more than one lead-generation element on your website.

You can increase your website's exposure and traffic by mentioning to website visitors and subscribers that you welcome the re-publishing of your content. As you can see in Figure 9.36, at the bottom of the home page next to a lead-generation element is a short blurb that encourages content republication: *"Republish ETR's Powerful Content on Your Website or Blog Without Charge! Get the no-hassle details, today!"*

Figure 9.35   *Multiple lead-gen elements and social media participation: Bly.com*

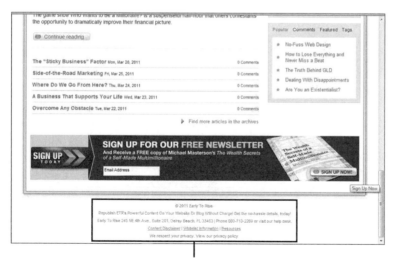

Statement to potential publishers that
this article may be freely republished

Figure 9.36   *Encourage content republication: EarlyToRise.com*

10

Dovetailing SONAR with Other High-Performing Internet Marketing Tactics

Over the years, I've had many responsibilities for the publishers I've worked for. One of the top priorities was list growth—building the free newsletter subscriber database with relevant, valid email addresses. As a savvy online marketer, I deployed many tactics that were proven and cost-effective.

First and foremost, I engaged in my SONAR marketing strategies to leverage the abundant content at my disposal. As you've read, SONAR touches upon several online tactics, including search engine optimization (SEO), search engine marketing (SEM), online PR, article marketing, and social media marketing (SMM).

Second, I coordinated reciprocal list swaps or guest editorials with fellow industry colleagues within my personal publishing contact network. Typically, a guest editorial or editorial contribution was a purely editorial article with an accompanying editorial note or byline directing the reader to the website for more information or to sign up for the e-newsletter. An ad swap was an e-newsletter sponsorship ad (text ad) encouraging readers to sign up for the free e-newsletter and touting some sort of free bonus report. This was reciprocated between publishers, so it was a fair promotional exchange. Ad swaps are at no "real" cost to either publisher (except use of the real estate of the newsletter, which is known as an opportunity cost). However, this tactic involves a couple variables:

- **It *is* who you know!**—You must have a network of synergistic publishers to reach out to, based on relationships that you've cultivated and people who know you. These are your first contacts when investigating a mutually beneficial opportunity for content or promotional sharing. You can certainly do your research and "cold email" synergistic publishers you don't know personally. But having an established relationship beforehand expedites the process. Try to network as much as possible at industry events and conferences, and build your own power network for potential marketing and editorial opportunities.

- **What's in it for me?**—What's in it for the publisher you're reaching out to? You need to have some leverage—something to exchange with the publisher—either great editorial or an attractive list size. This is particularly important if the publisher you're contacting isn't familiar with you. Ideally, your list size should be around the same as the publisher's you're reaching out to, to make the reciprocal exchange a level playing field.

> You need to have some leverage—something to exchange with the publisher—either great editorial or an attractive list size.

Finally, depending on my budget, I deployed online advertising, which might have consisted of pay-per-click (PPC), banner ads, text ads, and email/e-news sponsorship list rentals.

Joint Ventures, Affiliate Marketing, and Ad Swaps

Often your most synergistic and cost-effective opportunities will come from your friendly competitors. Smart businesses see the value in establishing and cultivating relationships with like-minded companies and publishers that have a similar target audience. They use this leverage for cross-promotional efforts, known in the industry as swaps for both sales and lead-generation (email-collection) efforts.

Networking at trade shows, conferences, and events, as well as searching the Web for synergistic websites, can open the door for advertising opportunities that have no out-of-pocket cost.

The trick is to use your list size, editorial content, or product as leverage to entice your potential partner. I say *partner* because you truly want someone whose product you believe in, so that you're in it for more than a one-off.

In addition to editorial related opportunities, such as guest editorials or editorial contributions, you can do revenue-generating efforts. The goal is to have a long-term, mutually beneficial, potentially lucrative arrangement—a win/win situation. Editorial and marketing arrangements between publishers work only if both parties are happy and are achieving their goals (which is usually making money in one way or another). If one party isn't getting the sales or email addresses it expected, the venture will cease. If the efforts are proving to be successful, you might want to schedule a rolling calendar with your publishing partner for either editorial or marketing initiatives every quarter, to keep the momentum going, and then cease when signs of performance fatigue appear.

When you're approaching a potential partner—or being approached by one—you want to ask some sample questions. These tips will show your partner-to-be that you're somewhat savvy about these types of arrangements and display your knowledge of the publishing industry.

 Note

Although you should always ask these questions (when applicable) to other publishers before committing to any editorial or marketing ventures, you should also be prepared to answer the same questions about your own company when necessary.

- **What is your list size?**—Usually the first and most basic question, this determines whether the effort is worth reciprocity. You want to make sure that your company and the one with which you are considering a partnership are on a level playing field. If another list is larger than yours, you can offer other incentives to sweeten the deal, such as better ad placement in the e-newsletter, an exclusive email, a larger revenue split percentage, or more frequent efforts (such as a two-for-one—you hit their list once, and they'll hit your list twice).

- **What percentage of your list (database) are buyers vs. free subscriptions?**—In other words, who are the customers who've purchased a product or service, and who are the prospects who've demonstrated interest (that is, free newsletter subscriber) but haven't purchased yet a product or service. This helps determine list viability and purchasing behavior by segmentation.

- **What's your AUS (average unit of sale)?**—What you are looking for here is the average sale and most common price point for all customers. In statistical terms, you're looking for both the mean (average) and the mode (most frequent). This helps you determine the purchasing power of the other company's list by dollar amount.

- **When was the last time you cleaned your list?**—This helps determine the integrity of the list—how "fresh" the list is and how many potential invalid emails or nonresponders are on it. If another publisher tells you its list has 50,000 names, but it hasn't cleaned the list in a year, you can estimate that about 10% of those emails are invalid.

- **What's your average open/click rate?**—This helps determine subscriber engagement—how well subscribers respond to the other publisher's email promotions or editorial communications.

- **Will you reciprocate a solo email and include a lift note?**—If you're negotiating a solo (dedicated) email between you and another publisher, it's important to make sure it's decided ahead of time if both sides will use a lift note. The lift note appears at the top of the email and comes from the host publisher—the company whose list your email will be going to. The purpose of the lift note is to *lift* overall response while warming up the reader to the company the email promotion is coming from (you!). When going to outside lists that don't necessarily know you and aren't familiar with your publication, products, or services, it's important to have a lift note before your promotional message so that subscribers don't view the cross-promotion as 'cold' or blindsiding them. The lift note is an implied endorsement by the subscriber, which helps boost your overall conversion rate.

- **Can you send me a sample of the creative you'd like to run for review/approval, as well as product sample?**—You want to see what kind of copywriting style the other publisher has and make sure you feel comfortable it sending to your readers. You also want to evaluate the product that might be cross-promoted before you recommend it to your readers. If you're not comfortable with the copy, most companies will work with you to make edits.

AFFILIATE MARKETING MUST HAVES

Affiliate marketing is a viable way to help build ancillary revenues by having someone else market your products. You can go about this through affiliate networks, such as Commission Junction or LinkShare, or simply start an affiliate program on your site and track it with affiliate programs or software such as DirectTrack or AffPlanet.

Before you start, make sure you know the critical elements to help grow your program:[1]

Promotion—This involves where you're promoting your program, at targeted locations and in recruiting affiliates to market your program. Make sure you list your program on all the top affiliate directories, networks, forums, associations, bulletin boards, websites, listings, and blogs. You also want to leverage free classified sites, such as Craigslist, and social media sites such as LinkedIn, which has several affiliate groups within the network. Of course, don't forget to create a powerful news release at the program's launch and to announce any important milestones.

Site awareness—Promoting your program on a site that doesn't have a decent traffic rank or web traffic is difficult. If your site has poor traffic, a professional affiliate marketer will look at it as a lost opportunity. This will only make his job harder.

Online store—Make sure to identify your best-selling and most universally appealing products. Those are the ones you want to have in your affiliate program. Also have varied price points: You don't want to pick prices too low, because, after the affiliate split, there won't be anything left. And you don't want to pick prices too high, since these will be a harder sale (because most affiliate marketing calls are cold calls). A good range is $50 to $300.

Affiliate rewards—Decide whether you're going to pay out per lead (PPL) or per sale. Decide whether you're going to have a flat commission rate or a tiered system. It's also good to consider if you're going to grant lifetime commissions (via a "cookie" to track and compensate on future sales) or pay affiliate for the original sale only. Do your competitive research and see what other, similar affiliate programs are paying out. Some of the best-performing programs on the Web are offering at least 25% of the product price.

Analytics—Make sure you have a robust reporting system. You want the ability to track underperformers and super affiliates (your top sales performers), and reward or incent accordingly through special offers or commissions. You also want to know which creatives are performing the best and worst, how many sales and leads are coming in, how long a lead is staying on the file, and the lifetime value of a lease (sales).

Keeping in touch—Top affiliate programs often have a newsletter or ongoing communication to keep their affiliates up-to-date on the latest products being offered, special sales incentives, updates to program terms, and other newsworthy notes.

---

1. Source: http://musclemarketing.blogspot.com/2009/06/affiliate-marketing-must-haves.html.

Affiliate marketing can help with nearly all of your online marketing objectives—lead generation, sales conversions, web traffic, branding, and buzz. Not having an affiliate marketing plan could be detrimental to your business.

Online Advertising: Tips and Tricks of the Trade

If you're thinking about testing online advertising, keep some important points in mind, to make sure you get the best bang for your buck. Take a look at some insider secrets of media buying.

Tip #1: Watch What's Happening in the Industry

Get subscriptions to free industry trade papers, such as *DM News*, *Response Magazine*, and *Target Marketing*, and as many free e-newsletters as you'd like.

 Note

I really like ClickZ.com because it's a leader in online marketing. Other online resources to consider are MarketingProfs.com, MarketingExperiments.com, MarketingSherpa.com, MarketingVox.com, AdRants.com, Mediabuyerplanner.com, and DoubleClick.com (which provides some of the industry's best practices, benchmarks, trends, and forecasts).

Tip #2: Research Which Ad Is a Higher Performer

If you're looking at online ads, whether it's a blog, website, or ad network, you'll find many to choose from (see Figure 10.1). But some banner ads perform better than others based on location and frequency to which it's served up (appears). Some popular banner ads include the following. For a complete list of banner ad sizes, visit http://www.iab.net/:

- Leader boards
- Skyscrapers
- Buttons
- Micro banners
- Large and medium rectangles

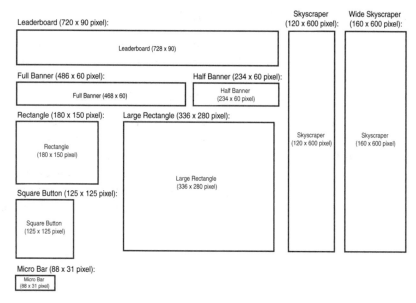

Figure 10.1 *Sample banner ad units. (Source: www.bannercreator.nu/banner-size.html)*

✉ *Note*

For more banner ads sizes, visit the Interactive Advertising Bureau (IAB) at www.iab.net/iab_products_and_industry_services/1421/1443/1452.

However, not every banner is created equal. For instance, my experience has shown that leader boards (ads that run horizontally across the top of a web page) or skyscrapers (ads that run vertically along the side of a web page) get the fewest clicks and conversions.

The best ad units and placements are typically large rectangles, such as 300×250, 250×250, or 336×300 IMUs (Internet marketing units). These are generally located above the page fold and within or close to the surrounding article content. As readers are perusing an article, their eyes can't help but notice the ad next to it—especially if you have a strong headline or eye-catching graphic image.

✉ *Note*

An eye-tracking study by The Poynter Institute showed that banner ads at the top left of the page—as well as ads close to the body of an article—received the most attention from readers.

Tip #3: Business Negotiations 101

In the process of putting together your media buy (or insertion order, as the official agreement is referred to), you will be required to analyze many proposals from different websites, blogs, or ad networks. You'll need to ascertain whether the rate you are being quoted is cost-effective and comparable to industry rates.

This is where a media tracking spreadsheet comes in handy. This will be a spreadsheet you create that contains all the websites, blogs, and ad networks you've reached out to, their contact information, the ad unit type and size, and the price. I recommend sorting this sheet by ad rate, lowest to highest, so that you can instantly see which contenders are out of budget or charging above the industry rate average. This document will help you have important information readily available at your fingertips, and you can then see which rates are comparable for which ad units.

 Note

When buying online ads, always ask for some kind of discount—whether it's because you're a first time buyer and you're testing online ads, or whether you're a frequent buyer and would like a volume discount. A good negotiator almost never pays rate card (the published price) for media. Also, when coordinating your media buy, see if you can get some goodwill extended such as free back-link on the publisher's Resources or similar page. This can aid in SEO efforts.

Keep in mind that when account executives start quoting you advertising rates, many drivers can influence that rate:

- **Seasonality**—Most web traffic typically drops during summer months and major holidays. Use this knowledge to your advantage and try to get lower rates during these times. You can also pause your ad if it happens to be running during a holiday and have it turned back on after the holiday.

- **Exclusivity**—Find out whether your ad is getting 100% of the rotations or is sharing that ad space with other advertisers. For instance, one banner ad location on a website might rotate and have five different messages each time you refresh. This is known as fixed ad placement or shared ad placement. If you're told that you have shared placement, find out how many actual impressions *you* will receive. Generally, shared ads are more cost efficient, though this depends on the size (popularity) of the website and whether your ad is fixed or shared. You sacrifice dedicated exposure, of course.

- **Site targeting**—Will your ad be ROS (run-of-site), by channel, or by page? Typically, you can drill down your banner ad or advertising message to a specific page. But the lower you drill, the more you pay for that targeting. The higher you go, the less you pay. ROS is the highest level, so it's usually the cheapest. Next is usually ROC (run-of-channel)—that is, running your ad within targeted sections of a site. You also can target specific pages or demographics. Your goals and budget determine which placement is best for your needs.

- **Remnant space**—Check with your account executive about remnant space (space that they're having difficulty selling for any reason) or last-minute specials. With more popular and high-traffic websites, you can get some great deals on remnant space. Make sure you know the terms and conditions.

- **Termination right**—Make sure that your insertion order has a termination right or "out clause" (typically 24 to 48 hours). This way, if you see after a week that your ad isn't performing, and you tested other ads, you can end the campaign without penalty and pay for only impressions served.

Tip #4: Due Diligence

If you're looking at placing a banner ad, make sure you gather demographic information and website analytics from the site where you're considering placing your ad. If you're considering renting an email list from a third-party, find out the size of its email list, how often the list gets mailed, the average unit sale per subscriber, and whether there will be a lift note (introduction memo/implied endorsement by the publisher). These variables help establish the value of the list.

Tip #5: Real-Time Reporting

Ask your account executive if you will have access to the online ad server (OAS) system or if you can get daily performance reports emailed to you. You want to look at impressions served, click-through rates, and open rates. These metrics illustrate the popularity of your ad and tell you whether it's resonating with website visitors. Are viewers clicking the banner but not converting at landing page? Are viewers visiting the page but not clicking the banner? Answers to these questions determine where you need to tweak your advertising creative.

- **High clicks (banner ad), low conversions (landing page)**—This typically indicates that something on the landing page isn't attractive to readers. Common reasons for low conversions include these:

    - The offer isn't enticing to the viewer.

    - The guarantee (return policy) isn't acceptable.

    - The price is too high.

    - The copy is not well written (your copy should be compelling and should draw the reader in).

    - There's no clear call to action (what exactly you want the reader to do next).

- **Low clicks (banner ad or text ad)**—This usually indicates that your front-end creative such as the banner or text ad isn't compelling or eye-catching. You have only a few seconds to grab the reader's attention. Great copywriting skills and/or strong graphical images are most important here.

Tip #6: Test Ad Networks

If your goal is to reach the biggest, broadest audience possible, and you want to run an ad on a few different websites, consider an ad network. Ad networks have arrangements with a variety of popular websites. Ad networks typically buy their ad units in bulk from the publishing sites, so the networks can pass the savings down to you. Some popular ad networks include Advertising.com and ValueClick.com. You can find a full list at iwebtool.com.

 Note

Make sure you get proposals from more than one network when researching your rates. Some of the lesser-known networks, such as BurstMedia.com, are extremely competitive with their rates and can really give the big guys a run for their money.

However, ask for a list of sample sites and find out how many total sites are in an ad network universe. Many ad networks might mention only their 5 top sites, but they might have a universe of 25 sites or more. The remaining 20 sites might be all tier II or tier III sites (otherwise known as microsites), with no real traffic or use to you. These are basically obscure sites on the fringe of the Internet—and they're certainly not worth more than a $1 per CPM (cost per thousand, which is a popular term of measurement for online ads).

Depending on how many impressions you buy and whether you're buying run-of-site or run-of-channel, your average cost for a large or medium rectangle banner ad can range from $2 to $9. For blog ads and blog networks, you can often find CPMs lower than $1. My preferred blog ad network is BlogAds.com. You can create your plan a la carte or buy "hives" (package of similar type blogs). Rates are affordable, and you can easily upload your creative and change as needed.

 Note

A great free tool that calculates CPM (cost per thousand) for you to help you figure out how many banner ad impressions you'll get as well as what your total cost would be can be found at http://www.clickz.com/cpm-calculator.

Tip #7: Don't Just Talk the Talk

When buying online media, confidence is king. Basic knowledge and the confidence to speak intelligently will go a long way. You need to be perceived as a savvy purchaser to the account executives you'll be dealing with. If you sound like you're unsure of yourself or like you don't know what you're talking about, don't be surprised if the ad exec tries to take advantage of you and get you to pay rate card, which is their published rate. When it comes to online media buying, practice and knowledge make perfect. Educate yourself. Read as many free online resources as possible about the subject matter. Use this book as a guide. Refer to the media tracking spreadsheet that you'll set up. A good way to put your toe in the water is to reach out to some ad networks for informational purposes. If you're not ready to buy, fine, but go through the process to see what it's like. The more you engage in online media buying, the better you'll be at it going forward.

> When buying online media, confidence is king.

Tip #8: Try to Get Goodwill Freebies for SEO

Whenever I do a media buy, I always see if I can get a courtesy back-link from the site I'm buying from—especially if they have a resource or links page. It's really no skin off their apple, and it's mutually beneficial for SEO. If the site you're buying from has a really strong traffic rank, it could be especially advantageous for you to get this back-link. More than half the time, I get it. The worst the account exec can say is no, so why not ask for it?

Tip #9: Buy More, Get More

If you have a larger ad budget (more than $5,000), you have some leverage to ask for some add-ons. For instance, if you're renting an email list of 100,000 names, see if the website or network will throw in a freebie—free banner ad or text ad for a week to test. Mention to the account executive that if this test performs well, you'll have a good reason to include this ad unit in the next media buy you do with them.

Media Cheat Sheet: "Must Know" Questions and Answers

When coordinating your insertion order (IO) with an online account executive, it's important to be prepared for some of the questions you'll be asked. Your response will determine the pricing and data presented in your overall proposal. Typical questions account execs might ask you include these:

- When do you want to start the campaign, and how long do you want it to run?
- What is the offer/goal (product sales, lead gen, other)?
- Do you have sample ad creative to send?
- What's your budget?
- What's your target audience (demographic, geographic, psychographic)?
- What kind of websites do you want your ad to run on (genre, category)?
- What type of ad unit are you interested in (size, placement)?

The more information you can provide, the more accurate your proposal, with costs, will be. Following are some other answers to know, to allow for leverage and leeway:

- **Budget**—I always tell account execs that it's a test buy and that my budget is small ($2,500 to $5,000). I tease them with an incentive, such as, "If this buy works, I'll roll out with bigger and more frequent buys." And why wouldn't I? If my ad makes money, it's a win/win situation. This usually helps the network be more flexible with their account minimum spending.
- **Out clause**—Many ad networks or websites won't mention an out clause. Be sure to insist on it. You want to be able to get out if the effort isn't working, without paying additional fees for doing so.

- **Payment terms**—Most, if not all, websites and networks will try to get you to pay with a credit card upfront. But I always like to ask for net 30 days payment terms and pay after the campaign is completed.

- **Ad units**—Let's say you're testing an LREC. Surprisingly, after one week, click-throughs are mediocre. If you don't have an alternate creative to run, see if the website or network can let you try the same creative, but in another ad unit, such as a text ad or skyscraper.

Online Public Opinion Polls for Editorial and Lead-Generation Success

One tactic that helped me build subscriber databases over the years was deploying online public opinion polls or surveys. Online polls are a viable way to bring in relevant, qualified email addresses. I've seen the right poll, with the right creative (headline copy), placed on the right websites generate in excess of 5,000 names in one month—in some cases, more than five times that!

To show the validity of the poll email addresses I had collected, I conducted a test in which I tracked a group of 5,000 poll participants. These people stayed on the file for up to six months—meaning they didn't opt out of the free e-newsletter they were automatically signed up for until after six months. These people were also active—meaning they were opening and clicking their e-newsletters and email correspondence, thereby engaging with the publisher. Six to nine months after the initial poll submission, fewer than 2% of the 5,000 names opted out of the free e-newsletter—that's fewer than 100 poll participants. This shows the quality of the lead, and a synergy between the poll question and the actual free editorial the poll participant received.

To quantify these results, when I divided my online media buy to help promote this poll by the number of total leads generated by the poll (poll participants), I got my cost per lead (CPL). My goal was to keep the CPL in the range of $1 to $10. So, in a nutshell, the poll campaign generated 5,000 leads within a few months. Fewer than 100 of those leads unsubscribed after more than six months. And the total cost per lead was under $10, which I thought was reasonable.

Polls can be placed internally (on your own website's home page) or externally (on another publisher's website or blog). And depending on where you place your poll (your media buy), this can also be a cost-effective strategy. For instance, I recommend testing almost any new banner ad creative on high-traffic, relevant blogs because they cost a fraction of the price of testing on a high-traffic website geared toward a similar audience.

The most important point to remember when using public opinion polls for enhanced editorial efforts is disclosure. You should clearly disclose to users before they submit a response that by taking the poll, they permit their email address to be collected, that the poll results will be published on your website or newsletter (which you should do), and that results might be shared with other media outlets (which you can do via a press release). Furthermore, you should make it clear to respondents that, to show your appreciation, participants will be automatically enrolled for a complementary subscription to your free e-newsletter (or receive a free bonus report), which they can opt out of at any time.

 Note

I also recommend having the link to your privacy policy or anti-spam policy close to the aforementioned disclosure statement; also mention, if applicable, that you do not rent or sell any email addresses collected.

Finding Customers in a Web 2.0 World

Web 2.0 isn't a newfangled Internet technology or software. And it's not a marketing tactic, per se. It's simply the evolution of the Internet into an environment of interactivity, reader participation, and usability. In effect, this changes users' web behavior. As Tim O'Reilly, founder of O'Reilly Media and the guy who coined the term "Web 2.0," puts it, it's "harnessing collective intelligence" through user-generated content.[2]

Web 2.0 opens up the dialogue between the user and the website or blog. This connection can help generate traffic and a viral buzz. Not all Web 2.0 traffic is a good thing. But from a search engine marketing standpoint, the benefits are clear and measurable. More traffic and frequent interactivity (or posts) equal better organic (free) rankings in search engine results.

Getting good organic rankings is a powerful way to find qualified prospective customers. A recent eye-tracking survey of people doing an Internet search showed that, 70% of the time, their eyes go to the upper-left side of the search results (the organic listings). Their eyes go to the right side of the search results (the paid listings) only 30% of the time.

Getting good organic rankings is a powerful way to find qualified prospective customers.

2. Source: Wendy Montes de Oca for Early to Rise. http://www.earlytorise.com/2008/02/22/how-to-find-customers-in-a-web-20-world/.

One way to increase your organic rankings—and take advantage of Web 2.0 user behavior—is with targeted online acquisition polls. Online polls can help you collect names and email addresses, gauge general market (or subscriber) sentiment, and generate sales via a redirect to a promotional page. They also allow for interactivity, enabling a user to sound off about a hot topic. I've been including polls in my online marketing strategy for at least six years now and have rarely been disappointed with the results.

Some websites, such as Surveymonkey.com, allow members to set up free or low-cost surveys and polls. However, they might not allow you to include a name-collection component or a redirect to a promotional offer. If that's the case, either ask your webmaster to build you a proprietary poll platform or use a poll script.

 Note

You'll find poll script examples at the following sites:

- hotscripts.com
- bgpoll.com/
- ballot-box.net/faq.php
- micropoll.com
- 2enetworx.com

You can help make your Web 2.0 poll a success in eight ways:

1. **Make it engaging**—Your poll question should engage the reader, encourage participation, pique interest, and tie into a current event. Be sure to have a comments field where people can make additional remarks. Sample topics include politics, the economy, health, consumer breakthroughs, the stock market, and foreign affairs. Sites that highlight the most-talked-about (and searched) topics on the Web include buzz.yahoo.com/, 50.lycos.com/, and google.com/press/zeitgeist.html.

2. **Be relevant**—Your poll question should also relate to your product, free e-zine topic, or free bonus report topic. This will greatly improve your conversion rate (the number of people who actually participate in your poll) and your up-sell rate. Let's say that your free offer is a sign-up for an investment e-zine, and your up-sell is a redirect landing page promotion for a paid investment newsletter. In that case, your poll question should be something like, "Do you think the Dow will rise or fall in 2011?"

3. **Offer an incentive**—After people take your poll, tell them that, to thank them for their participation, you're automatically signing them up for your free e-zine or e-alerts, which they can opt out of at any time. To reduce the number of bogus email addresses you get, offer a free "must read" e-report, too. Assuming that it's your policy not to sell or rent email names to third parties (and it should be), indicate that next to the sign-up button. This will reassure people that it's safe to give you their email address.

4. **Tag the responses**—Having your poll question somehow tie into your product line makes the names you collect extremely qualified for future offers. Each name should be tagged by your database folks according to the answer they gave. Segmenting the names into such categories will make it easier for you to send targeted offers to them later.

   Let's say that your product line includes an investment e-zine on equities. In that case, your poll question might ask people which investment product they think has the best returns: money market, gold, equities, or options. Those who answer "equities" will be prime candidates for a promotion for the e-zine.

5. **Use the results for new initiatives**—In addition to collecting names, online polls help you gauge general market opinion—and could help you come up with new products. Keeping with our previous example, you would flag all the responses that come in. If an overwhelming number of responders indicate an interest in an investment product you don't have—maybe one on gold—you should consider developing one. You now have an instant market of people to sell that product to.

6. **Strengthen your new relationships**—You need to reinforce the connection between the poll people just participated in and your e-zine or e-alerts. Make sure each name that comes in gets an immediate "thank you" (for taking the poll). Then send an automatically generated email with the link for the downloadable free e-report you promised. Consider sending a series of "bonding" emails, too. These emails help them get to know who you are, what you do, and how you can benefit them. This also helps improve their lifetime customer value.

7. **Gratify participants with the results**—Don't leave poll participants hanging—tell them that you'll publish the results in your free e-zine or on your website (to encourage them to check it regularly). This can increase readership and website traffic.

8. **Publish the best reader comments**—On your poll landing page, mention that you might publish some user feedback (anonymously) in your e-zine or on your website. Pick the very best, most powerful responses to use. Republishing user feedback is fundamental to the Web 2.0 concept, and it has been extremely successful for social networking communities and blogs.

Marketers have used polls to collect names for years. However, with the recent surge in (and buzz about) Web 2.0, you should include polls in your online marketing mix now more than ever.

Public opinion polls aren't just for finding new customers (lead generation), either. They allow you to measure customer sentiment, which, in turn, can affect customer retention and service.

Polls can also be used for cross-selling. As you can see in Figure 10.2, a poll can be used to bring in new leads as well as qualify those leads in the form of the answer selections on the poll landing page, then redirect the poll participant to the appropriate sales offer. A qualified lead may be redirected to a promotional landing page somehow tied to the poll topic or theme. An unqualified lead may receive a completely different offer—one that is more generic and evergreen in nature—but appealing as a front-end (entry level) product.[3]

Pubic opinion polls are one of the best editorial vehicles I've used to gauge market interest and build a free newsletter list. Questions asked and answers received can help you on your product development efforts. They're interactive, fun, and they allow people to sound off about various topics. And you'll see once you start reviewing results that some participants are quite passionate about their viewpoints.

> Pubic opinion polls are one of the best editorial vehicles I've used to gauge market interest and build a free newsletter list.

Sadly, many marketers underestimate and misunderstand the true value of a poll or survey. If done correctly, polls and surveys can be a completely viable and reliable way to build your prospect database, measure sentiment, and increase sales.

---

3. Source: Wendy Montes de Oca for Early to Rise. http://www.earlytorise.com/2008/02/22/how-to-find-customers-in-a-web-20-world/.

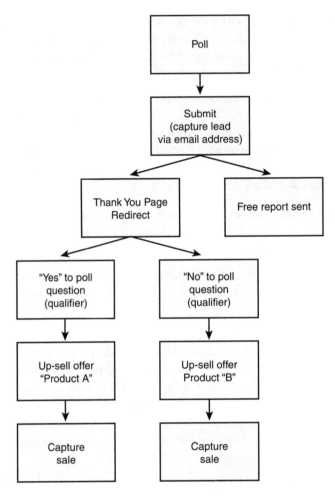

Figure 10.2   *The online poll process flow.*

Polls can also be used internally or externally—that is, either on your own website as an alternate way to collect email address, or placed on other websites/blogs via banner or text ads through a media buy.

As mentioned earlier, it's important to have full disclosure about the poll before participants cast their vote. This is a best practice from an anti-spam viewpoint, and it also sets participant expectations. By doing this, you reduce your opt-out, bounce, spam report, and non-open rate. Put the disclosure statement on the landing page immediately before the Submit button. It should illustrate that the participant's email address is safe and will be used for a free newsletter subscription. Here's a standard poll disclosure statement:

Your email privacy is assured. We will never sell or rent your email address to third parties. As a gift for participating in the poll, you will receive a free bonus report and subscription to our newsletter, which you can unsubscribe from at any time. Votes with invalid emails will not be counted. Poll results will be published on our website and/or e-newsletter. Tell us what you think! We look forward to hearing from you. Various media outlets and others may be interested in poll results as well. Vote today!

The last sentences of the poll disclosure encourages return visits to the website and explains that, with the free e-newsletter subscription, subscribers will have a chance to see poll results.

Variables for online poll success will vary based on the following:

- The poll question(s) you use—how well the question or questions attract and resonate with your target prospects

- The placement of the poll (relevant, targeted blogs, websites)

- The amount of media purchased

- Your overall advertising budget

A great cost-effective way to test polls is to buy banner ads on targeted blogs that are popular and have high traffic. These blogs are a fraction of the cost of the typical mainstream websites.

However, it's important to note that unless you have an up-sell landing page that comes up immediately after completion of the poll, your leads will not be initially monetized. This means that if you don't have an up-sell page after you get the lead, you won't see this lead convert into a paying customer for a few months. The typical sales cycle is 30 to 120 days, depending on overall market conditions and product price points.

To some, initial monetization is important, to offset the media buy. To others, having those names convert organically in the normal sales cycle of 30 to 120 days is fine, as long as they can track back that customer to the original point of entry—the poll. If you opt for the organic conversion approach, make sure you segment poll participants and follow up with a separate email campaign for bonding and sales conversion within the first month of poll participation.

INCORPORATING SEO BEST PRACTICES INTO YOUR WEBSITE

Search engine optimization (SEO) is an important way for visitors to find your website organically—that is, for your website to appear in organic search results.[4]

Many companies, large and small, spend much time and effort working on SEO best practices to help increase awareness and visibility, as well as to drive website traffic. Having a website without SEO is like having a storefront business with no signage. People simply won't find you.

On the other hand, having SEO but not implementing it effectively or correctly can hurt your business *and* your website's exposure. Google and other search engines monitor such activity and take action accordingly if they find websites that violate industry best practices and ethical standards.

It's important for business owners and their online marketers to understand SEO best practices and "white hat" versus "black hat" SEO tactics.

In a nutshell, think of the old Westerns, in which the bad guys wore black and good guys wore white. "Black hat" SEO tactics are the "bad" or frowned-upon tactics, such as keyword stuffing, meta tag spamming, link farming (buying unrelated, irrelevant back links to your website), hidden content (white text that the human eye can't read but search engines can), doorway or gateway pages, and more.

"White hat" SEO tactics are the "good" or accepted tactics, such as relevant keywords, content, tagging, and back-links, as well as targeted and unique URLs for each page of the website.

To avoid potential penalties (such as temporary suspension or removal from organic search results listings), make sure your SEO or web marketing person is one of the good guys. Make sure that your SEO also keeps up on the latest in SEO news and trends.

---

4. Source: http://advertising.about.com/od/onlineadvertising/a/whitehatvsblackhatseo.htm.

11

How to Write Great, Free Content (That Gets Read and Passed Around!)

Throughout this book, I've given my personal insight on how to create great content that gets leveraged—and read—using the SONAR Content Distribution Model™.

However, I also want to share knowledge from some of the top online publishers in the industry. At a recent publishing conference, the world's best publishers met and shared editorial trends on what's working and what's not with readers. Although these publishers come from various industries, there are some fundamental tips that apply across the board.

One of the main topics of discussion was how to write great free e-zine content. Take a look at the top 10 takeaways:

1. **Be relevant**—Try to segment your audience by interest—one-to-one outperforms one-to-many every time. If you have data on your subscribers, use it to your advantage.

2. **Be dynamic**—Use personal touches and remind the recipients why you're writing to them.

3. **Employ a creative strategy**—This plays well to how well your e-zine performs. Keep newsletter articles short, sweet, and to the point—ideally, no more than two scrolls deep and no more than 650 pixels wide.

4. **Humanize your content**—It's Pavlovian—we always see links that read "'Add us to your address book" or "'View web version.'" Try to soften that call to action, as if you are talking face-to-face with the reader.

5. **Be transparent**—Don't make readers try to figure out what to do next—tell them plainly. Your primary call to action directing readers to their next step (if there is one) should be both above *and* below the fold. This is a great way to bond with subscribers by linking to more information or for cross-selling opportunities, tying one of your products into your editorial content. Use an action verb; make it stand out (make it bold); and be consistent with the objective, content, and subject line of surrounding content.

   > Don't make readers try to figure out what to do next—tell them plainly.

6. **Consider location, location, location**—Your readers will make up their minds in less than two seconds about what they will do with your e-zine: Read it completely or close the issue. Treat the top 2 to 4 inches of your e-zine as the most valuable real estate on the page, and use it accordingly. Reserve this location for content that will grab the readers and get them to share the issue with others or "like" the issue.

7. **Show innovation**—Make sure you can accommodate the mobile device that is rendering your copy. This medium is becoming wildly popular, and you want to be able to reach your readers on all media.

8. **Share with your network (SWYN)**—Make sure you have the functionality in place to support and maintain a viral growth strategy. This will give your content legs to increase your brand's exposure and visibility.

Also, have a brief message in your content that encourages readers to share the information or forward it to a friend. This should be easy to do with a click of the mouse. If you have a content syndication policy, clearly disclose in your newsletter that it's okay to republish content, as long as the publisher/author gets full attribution and a back-link to the main article on your website.

9. **Be reader friendly**—Lay out your content in a brief and easy-to-read manner. Use bullets, short paragraphs, and keyword-rich subheadings to help readers scan content quickly and find key information rapidly. Make sure there's ample white space between paragraphs, to make it easy on the eyes and prevent content clutter.

10. **Use links**—Whether they're used to encourage readers to forward to a friend, to state your privacy policy, to encourage readers to white-list you, to handle subscription management, or, yes, even to allow readers to opt out, using links is a simple way to help readers find your content and pass it around. It's also subscriber-centric and a great way to empower readers to manage how—and whether—they want to receive your information.

What makes great content? Publishers and editors have been asking themselves that question for years. Although many tips are staples, new recommendations accompany each new technological advancement that alters the way people like to receive their content.

Information is moving quickly. Trends are changing rapidly. Sometimes you need to take a deep breath, slow down, and evaluate things from a more intuitive level.

Don't be afraid to take a leap with your readers and give them the information they want in the best way *they* prefer to receive it. Don't guess—get it straight from the horse's mouth.

Survey your subscribers at least once a year, to keep abreast of their likes, dislikes, preferences, and competitive interests, as well as to gather other relevant demographic, geographic, and psychographic data.

"Know your list" is a mantra that can't be stressed enough when it comes to having a successful, free e-zine.

Industry Viewpoints

In this section, I share some additional viewpoints from industry friends and colleagues. These folks are top publishers in their niches. They know what it takes to write great content that not only gets read, but also gets passed around.

Note

The following tips come from some editorial and publishing masters of their game. The information here is presented in their words.

Michael Masterson, Publisher, Agora, Inc., Early to Rise

There are all kinds of e-zines—even all kinds of business models that use e-zines differently. Each has its own readership, with different expectations regarding content, but some rules apply to all e-zine content:

1. **The quality of the ideas presented is paramount**—A reader may sign up for an e-zine for many different reasons, but he will continue to read it only if he feels that his time invested in reading is yielding valuable ideas. *Valuable* in this context means provocative, memorable, and useful. Use these three criteria to judge the content, and you won't miss the mark.

2. **Less is better than more**—If you overwhelm the reader with ideas—even valuable ideas—he will come away from the reading experience emotionally neutralized. That happens because the reader recognizes subconsciously that he has taken in more information than he can possibly act upon. Being comprehensive, therefore, is not the virtue some writers and publishers think it is.

3. **Specificity is key**—Unsubstantiated claims and promises may attract your readers' attention, but you will never win their trust unless you back up those claims and promises with specifics.

4. **Stories sell the heart**—Facts sell the brain. Don't forget that the job of good writing is as much to appeal to the readers' emotional intelligence as it is to provide them with rational evidence.

Jason Holland, Managing Editor, Agora, Inc., Early to Rise

It may seem ordinary or boring. But one of the most important elements for great newsletter content (or any communication with your customers) is the Flesch–Kincaid readability score. At Early to Rise, our benchmark is an FK score of 7.5 or less. We've found that this encourages writers to use clean, easily understandable language. That means few big words you have to look up in a dictionary, and it eliminates run-on sentences that you have to read several times to understand. At first, writers chafe at this restriction. They say it hampers creativity. But we stick to it because it makes reading an ETR essay a joy, not a chore. By the way, this paragraph scores a 7.5. The FK/readability score is a feature in Microsoft Word. Several websites also offer this service.

Brian Kurtz, Executive Vice President, Boardroom, Inc., Bottom Line Secrets

When I describe our model to people, I always say it's "free, great, usable content with some advertising" rather than "advertising with some content." We call the recipients "subscribers," and we treat them as if they were paid. We develop a personal relationship with them through our personalities (the authors of the editorial product). We talk about having "six newsletters, three print and three online," and we talk about the free e-letters with the same enthusiasm as the paid print newsletters. We never diminish the value of the editorial we deliver, whether it's free or paid. Our open rates for our e-letters and online newsletters are fantastic, from what I hear in the industry, and I think this commitment to quality keeps folks opening, subscribing, and eventually buying our fantastic products. If there is one rule of thumb for us, it's that delivering the best content, whether free or paid, should never be compromised.

Christopher Ruddy, President and CEO, Newsmax Media, Inc.

Here are some ideas about e-zines that have worked for Newsmax:

1. **Keep the subject line simple and powerful**—Subject lines are extremely important for readers to have any interest in opening their email and to feel like they're getting consistently important messages worth their time and effort. We cover politics, and I like subject lines that have drama and simplicity. The subject line should have a subject, an active verb, and an object—for example, "Obama Defends His Record" is a powerful subject line.

2. **Information in e-zines should not be information that the reader has already heard or seen**—For instance, we avoid news headlines that are widely reported by other news agencies. We like to have unique information, making readers feel that they are getting valuable content and that their time is well spent reading our emails.

3. **Avoid images**—We are not big fans of heavy images. Occasionally we use a photo or image if we want to bring home a point, but we find that text readers are interested in information; images sometimes hurt the processing of information. Again, keep it simple.

4. **More is better**—We send out multiple emails every day. We find that if you're sending interesting content, readers have a high tolerance for receiving emails, as long as they know that it's something they're not getting from other communication channels and that we're not wasting their time.

Steve Kroening, Editor, Soundview Publications, Inc., Second Opinion Newsletter, Women's Health Letter, and Real Cures

In real estate, it's location, location, location. In great e-zines, it's solutions, solutions, solutions. Whether it's your subject line promising a solution, your first sentence teasing the solution, or your copy delivering and proving the solution, it's all about solutions to big problems. The bigger the problem and the better the solution, the more people you'll persuade to open your e-zine.

Alice Wessendorf, Managing Editor, Healthier Talk

The key to producing great content that resonates and gets read in today's social web environment boils down to one word: honesty. Believe in what you're writing—in what you're doing—or the readers *will* see through it and you *will* fail. If you're honest and transparent with your readers—regardless of whether you're writing about the latest Big Pharma scandal or a great new supplement they should try—they will reward you. Your agenda when writing should always be first to make a *connection* with the reader, and the success will naturally follow.

Sean Brodrick, Natural Resource Analyst, Uncommon Wisdom Daily, Weiss Research, Inc.

1. **Write about things people are passionate about**—For example, when I write about geopolitics in the Middle East, people yawn. When I write about gold, that really attracts eyeballs, and it's much more likely to get tweeted.

2. **Offer readers a voice and respond to them**—Too many websites follow the old media pattern of just talking to their readers. When readers can talk back, they get much more interested. And when readers get quoted or see themselves responded to, they become loyal readers. They're much more likely to pass around something they have a voice in, even if it's only in the comments section.

3. **Eye candy**—I don't mean girls in bikinis. I mean charts and graphics. If you can crystallize your point with a chart or a graphic, that's something that people will seize on to email to their friends or post on Twitter or Facebook.

4. **Be contrarian (but be honest)**—If you can make a statement that no one else is making, it's much more likely to get a response and get passed around. But whatever you say must be honest—you can't say something just for the sake of generating controversy or being a contrarian. Smart readers can sniff out a phony, and they'll point out inconsistencies.

Dr. Jonny Bowden, Publisher, In Step with Jonny: Straight Talk Nutrition for the 21st Century

Never overestimate your readers' attention span. It's utterly amazing how many things get misread, misinterpreted, and misunderstood. Write clear, concise sentences and short paragraphs. Newsletter writing is fundamentally different from book writing. I frequently take a paragraph of 300–400 words that would have worked fine in a book and break it up into three paragraphs of 100 or so words, just to make it visually interesting and easier to scan. People seem to respond to headlines that stress danger, uncover secrets, or tease the reader in some way. They also love numbered lists.

Examples:

- "This food can help prevent breast cancer!"
- "Are you making 1 of the 4 top mistakes in money management?"
- "This ingredient in toothpaste can kill you!"
- "Learn the secret of living longer, from the longest-lived people in the world"

Remember, 10 zillion things are competing for your readers' attention—you want to give them a reason to click through. Curiosity is a good one. Much like with Tweets, there seems to be an ideal proportion of info-only messages to product-promotion messages. In a newsletter of three stories, I make two of them purely informational and use the third to deliver information that is subtly linked to a product. For example, the story might be on some new benefit for vitamin D; when vitamin D is mentioned, I link to my vitamin D product in the store.

I think the most important tip of all is one that can be summed up in a quote by the great screenwriter William Goldman: "Nobody knows anything." Internet marketing is still the Wild, Wild West, and despite a million "studies" by marketers, there really isn't a coherent, accepted literature on what gets people to open and buy. On some level and to some degree, we're all still guessing. Be willing to experiment, learn, and change course. Use your instincts, but listen to people who know what they're talking about (they're out there—they're just hard to find sometimes). To paraphrase the famous saying, "Trust your gut, but verify." Be true to yourself. Some people are perfectly comfortable with marketing strategies that include screaming headlines promising amazing results, huge amounts of weight lost, huge amounts of money made, and so on. If you're not comfortable with these tactics and they don't reflect who you are, do something else. Your readers will respond to what's authentic.

Bob Bly, Publisher, The Direct Response Letter, CTC Publishing

People want valuable, how-to information that solves a specific problem (for example, how to get a job, pay for college, etc.). Use short, practical tips. When e-mailing your list, at least 50% of the messages should be content, not sales copy. Make sure that you include actionable items readers can use right away. Write copy in a natural, friendly, conversational style, like one friend talking to another. Use short sentences, short paragraphs, and short words. Keep it simple. Include examples of how your advice can be put into real-world application. Use your own experience as a primary reference source rather than merely rewriting someone else's content in your own words, as so many do on the Internet.

12

Best SONAR Platforms and Measuring Success

When you're thinking about online marketing resources and potential SONAR platforms, you'll never find a shortage of locations for uploading your content. Endless websites, blogs, forums, directories, and message boards are at your fingertips.

However, when it comes to SONAR working at its best, it really boils down to matching up the right message with the right medium—in other words, as I mentioned throughout in this book, look for sites that are relevant to your target audience, relevant to your content, and with a respectable traffic rank that illustrates site popularity and visits.

It's much better to disseminate your content and messages on 10 highly ranked, highly relevant sites than 110 irrelevant sites with no website visibility. This is the epitome of quality versus quantity.

Every business's SONAR platforms are unique to their needs. And because I've been using SONAR for years for different companies, as well as for my consulting clients in numerous niches, I have hands-on knowledge of which sites generate the best results for the SONAR Content Distribution Model™.

Of course, I strongly recommend that you conduct your own research on which SONAR platforms are ideal for you, to find the right combination of relevance and rank.

Conducting your specific SONAR due diligence simply involves doing Internet searches to determine which sites are ideal for your needs. This involves basic web searches using similar terms as these:

> It's much better to disseminate your content and messages on 10 highly ranked, highly relevant sites than 110 irrelevant sites.

- Top/best [insert your niche] content syndication networks or top/best [insert your niche] article submission sites

- Top/best [insert your niche] free online press distribution services

- Top/best [insert your niche] social bookmarking sites or top/best [insert your niche] social communities

- Top/best [insert your niche] article directories

- Top/best [insert your niche] blogs

- Top/best [insert your niche] message boards

- Top/best [insert your niche] forums

When you find five relevant sites in each SONAR platform that you're interested in, check out the site's page (traffic) rank at Alexa.com and/or Compete.com, to get an idea of site popularity. Many of your search results may contain top lists, such as "top 25 marketing blogs," in which publishers have included the Alexa traffic rank or Google page rank in their lists. This is a great starting point because it accomplishes most of your work. What remains is repurposing your content, following the SONAR strategy as indicated in this book, and going through some good ol' trial and error.

However, if you're looking for honest insight on what worked for me, you're in luck. The following are my favorite sites; I've had fantastic results with them and highly recommend checking them out.

Note

Just to be clear, I am not affiliated in any way with any of these sites, nor am I receiving any compensation or affiliate commission for mentioning them. It's my own, personal opinion based on my SONAR experience and performance.

So without further ado, here are my favorite SONAR platforms in alphabetical order:

- **Amazines.com**—Popular article directory. Allows members to set up and upload content for multiple authors.

- **Amazon.com**—Great location if your focus is using SONAR for a book launch. Offers targeted forums and discussion boards to generate buzz and visibility.

- **AmericanChronicle.com**—Article directory/content syndication. Syndicates content to regional sister sites such as the California Chronicle, Los Angeles Chronicle, and World Sentinel.

- **ArticleBase.com**—Popular article directory. Allows members to set up and upload content for multiple authors.

- **ArticlesFactory.com**—Popular article directory.

- **Articles.Mercola.com**—Popular community for well-known alternative health doctor Joseph Mercola. Allows members to submit articles.

- **Big-Boards.com**—Largest message board on the Web with tons of sub-categories in their directory for most every niche you can think of.

- **BizSugar.com**—Social media website where small businesses can upload news, blog posts, press releases, and other important information.

- **Buzzle.com**—Article directory/content syndication platform. Typically gets good organic exposure.

- **Craigslist.com**—Technically, Craigslist is more of a directory of services than a content site, per se. But you can create targeted messages in the classifieds section, driving traffic to content or other promotional pages. You also can target your message based on geography and topic of interest.

- **Digg.com**—Popular social bookmarking site.

- **e-Healtharticles.com**—Article directory targeted for its health-related content.

- **Ezinearticles.com**—The granddaddy of all article-marketing sites. Allows you to add various authors if you publish content for more than one guru.

- **Facebook.com**—The top dog of social media communities, with more than 500 million active members. I prefer Facebook to Twitter because it allows a higher character count for content posts and other SONAR messages.

- **FastPitchNetworking.com**—Social network where business professionals can upload news, events, press releases, blog posts, and more.

- **FinancialSense.com**—Investing website that permits editorial submissions. Contributors get a byline on the Contributor's List.

- **Forums.ivillage.com**—Popular forum with important topics that are geared toward women, such as pregnancy, parenting, health, entertainment, beauty, home, and love.

- **Free-Press-Release.com**—Free online press release platform that offers good visibility and pick-up (syndication) by bloggers and online news aggregators. Has an admin page where you can view press release hits.

- **GoArticles.com**—Popular article directory.

- **HealthierTalk.com**—Great health and news community for publishers to submit content, and offers a bio page for authors, which is ideal for credibility and increased brand awareness and SEO (link building).

- **i-Newswire.com**—Free online press release platform that offers good visibility and pick-up (syndication) by bloggers and online news aggregators. Allows only one free release per week.

- **LibertyNewsForum.com**—Good political forum.

- **LinkedIn.com**—Powerful professional networking community where you can participate in discussions, share content, and offer expert advice. Groups reflect virtually every interest, from A to Z.

- **More.com/Community/Forums**—Popular women's site with high-traffic forum.

- **NewsNation.net/Forum**—Good political forum.

- **PoliticalForum.com**—Good political forum.

- **Politico.com**—High-traffic political forum.

- **PRLog.org**—My favorite PR site! Free online press release platform that offers good visibility and pick-up (syndication) by bloggers and online news aggregators. Has an admin page where you can view press release hits.

- **SeekingAlpha.com**—Top finance and investing blog that permits content submissions.

- **SelfGrowth.com**—High-traffic, popular content syndication site where you can upload articles or websites (for back-links). Focuses on various topics, including success, relationships, finances, business health, mental health, spirituality, lifestyle, and more.

- **StumbleUpon.com**—Popular social bookmarking site.

- **Squidoo.com**—Publishing platform where you can create web pages, or "lenses," that act as satellite sites, to increase visibility and drive traffic to your website or promo page.

- **Topix.com**—Site with various forums to start discussions or create buzz.

- **Twitter.com**—Another popular social site. Great for short posts that link to a landing page with the full message. Posts can go viral easily with retweets. It's a nice complement to Facebook, if you don't have overlap in your friends and followers.

- **WarriorForum.com**—Top forum for most things business. Great for marketers, entrepreneurs, business owners, freelancers, and copywriters.

Gauging Your SONAR Results

As you've read in this book, you've found that content is king—and it *is* cash. Using the SONAR Content Distribution Model™ can help you leverage your words and turn them into something that can actually boost your business—whether it's as a sales tool or through increased website visibility, traffic, brand awareness, lead generation, subscriber bonding, or industry credibility.

SONAR is a proven method that works time and time again. And that's because, if you have good content, people will want to read it. When you offer valuable content for free, people will relate to you on a deeper level and you'll achieve the golden tripod, or what my friend Dr. Karen Keller likes to call LBT (like, bond, trust).

LBT can do wonders for your company and create a loyal community of subscribers that will generate sales and referral business. But don't just take my word for it or rely on the performance of the case studies in this book. Test SONAR for yourself. With your own content and this book as your guide, you are now armed with the tools needed to implement and replicate the SONAR Content Distribution Model™.

However, before you start, it's important to create a "website progression chart" for pre- and post-SONAR data review. This baseline can effectively gauge where you started and show your post SONAR results.

Before you initiate your SONAR efforts, create a simple spreadsheet in Excel or a table in Word, and note a few critical benchmarks. Table 12.1 shows what your chart should look like and the data that's needed so you can compare results.

As you can see in Table 12.1, the progression chart sets a baseline then measures progress.

Table 12.1   Sample Benchmark and Progression Chart

	Month 1	Month 2	Month 3	Comments
U.S. traffic ranking				Global traffic source: http://www.alexa.com/
Monthly website site visits (traffic)	YTD average: Monthly average:	YTD average: Monthly average:	YTD average: Monthly average:	Source: Google Analytics
Current e-newsletter subscribers				This shows lead-generation growth.
Website back-links				Sources: www.backlinkwatch.com This shows content syndication and viral marketing.
Number of organic search results for your brand keywords (that is, website name, publication name, and author name)				Source: Google.com This shows visibility and exposure.

	Month 1	Month 2	Month 3	Comments
Average visitor time on site (minutes)				Source: Google Analytics
				This shows visitors' interest in site content.
				Note: Average visitor "peruses" between 3–5 minutes.
YTD website sign-ups (leads collected through your website sign-up page)				This shows lead-generation growth.
				Note: Several variables might affect this number, including, but not limited to, inclusion of Google Analytics to sign-up page (to see "goals" or conversions), number of lead gen sign-up elements on the home page, variety of lead gen elements on the sign-up page (that is, public opinion polls), placement of the lead gen element on the sign-up page, copy of lead gen landing page, and use of incentive for sign up (that is, free report).
YTD website sign-ups (leads collected through your targeted lead-generation page)				This shows lead-generation growth.

	Month 1	Month 2	Month 3	Comments
Total current partners (#) (rev share/lead gen)				This shows the number of any affiliate or JV partners that may have been leveraged through content syndication.
Current partner leads (#) and sales ($) (avg. per month)				This shows number of leads and dollar amount of sales generated by any affiliate or JV partners that may have been leveraged through content syndication.
Avg. revenue per weekly e-zine ($)				This shows total avg. weekly sales (monetization) from free e-newsletter, such as text ads, banner ads, affiliate ads, and editorial notes.
Total current year website revenues ($)				This shows total sales (monetization) from website/organic traffic.
Avg. revenue per subscriber ($)				This shows avg. sales (monetization) from editorial; that is, e-zine per subscriber. Formula: Total number of subscribers div./revenues.
YTD total sales ($) (from e-newsletter)				This shows sales (monetization) from editorial; that is, e-zine.

The purpose of Table 12.1 is to be a high-level report where you can easily see growth. From this report, you can also spin-off more detailed direct response reports that track and measure specific email promotions, e-newsletter issues, and other marketing efforts. Direct response metrics that would be important to include are the following:

- Subject line
- Date deployed
- Day of week deployed
- In-house or external (if external, the vendor or list name)
- Source code (if you have the ability to track by number)
- Type of effort (that is, solo email, banner ad, text ad, etc.)
- Type of effort (that is, sales or lead generation)
- Total audience size/circulation
- CPM (cost per thousand, if applicable)
- Total cost
- Opens (#)
- Open rate (%)
- Clicks (#)
- Click-through rate (%)
- Total leads generated
- Response rate (%)
- Conversion rate (%)
- Cost per lead (CPL)
- Return on investment (ROI)
- Revenue per name ($)

Of course, although SONAR is powerful, it's not magic. Success won't happen overnight, and it won't make you millions by itself. SONAR is a cost-effective, proven strategy to complement your existing marketing mix.

If you're looking to save money using relatively free organic methods such as SONAR to increase reach, visibility, traffic, leads, buzz, and sales, also remember to balance expediency with budget. Nearly any tactic that is free will take longer than paid advertising. SONAR could take several weeks or months

SONAR could take several weeks or months to gain momentum and give you a foothold in the organic search results...but it will happen.

to gain momentum and give you a foothold in the organic search results...but it will happen.

If implemented correctly and added as a standard tactic to your weekly online marketing efforts, SONAR will make a substantial difference in your business's growth.

Just make sure you use your progression chart as a reference point, and keep your expectations realistic. I'm confident that you won't be disappointed with the results.

Much luck and success!

Glossary: Key Terms to Know When Deploying SONAR or Any Online Marketing Strategy

While you are reading this book—as well as when you are implementing most any online marketing strategy (including the SONAR Content Distribution Model™)—you will come across frequently used terms you might not be familiar with. The following are some of the most commonly used terms among online marketers and industry professionals to help you better understand key terms and concepts in this book. Also, knowing and understanding these terms will help you become a more educated and savvy online marketer—which is a critical step in learning and mastering any strategy.

Account Executive—This is your key point person at the online ad agency who coordinates your insertion order (advertising contract) when you are buying online media. This person will handle your customer service needs as well as help get you critical performance data regarding your campaign.

Ad Swap—Also known as reciprocal ad swap or list swap. An ad swap is when two publishers agree to cross-promote to each other's lists (subscribers). This can be done via e-newsletters or through direct emails. Each publisher includes the other publisher's ad or promotion in their newsletter or email and then sends it to their list. There is no sharing or renting of subscriber email addresses.

Advertising Metrics—Measureable data used to define marketing performance such as click-through rate (CTR), conversion rate, cost-per-click (CPC), cost-per-action (CPA), and cost per thousand (CPM).

Alexa Page Rank—A website company that ranks other websites and assigns a traffic/page rank. The lower the rank (number), the better the website traffic. Many media buyers use Alexa Page Rank as a gauge for determining whether they want to purchase ad placement on a particular site and loosely gives an idea on the website's popularity (visits).

Average Unit of Sale (AUS)—A direct response measurement that is simply the average sale and most common price point among your total list size. In statistical terms, it's looking for both the "mean" (average) and the "mode" (most frequent). This figure helps determine the purchasing power of the other company's list by dollar amount. The formula for calculating your average unit of sale is to divide your total amount of sales (in dollars) by your total list size.

Back-Linking—A search engine marketing tactic that simply means your content has been republished or syndicated on another website or blog and links back to your website—the original content source.

Banner Ad Units—Graphic images used on websites to advertise a product or service. There are a variety of popular sizes. The Interactive Advertising Bureau (IAB) has a full list of current and delisted ad units at www.iab.net/iab_products_and_industry_services/1421/1443/1452.

Black Hat SEO—These are unethical and frowned-upon search engine marketing practices that are used to trick search engines into bestowing a better search ranking upon site. Not only are black hat tactics unethical—in some cases, they are illegal—they also can actually negatively affect a website's organic ranking—and could cause your site to not show up in search results at all. Black hat SEO tactics include hidden content, keyword stuffing, link farming, content farming, and door-way/gateway pages that are used to trick search engines (algorithms) into thinking a low-quality site is actually more popular than it is. I don't advocate any black hat tactics, and you should steer clear from those who do.

Branding—A form of marketing in which a consumer sees or hears your message (albeit email, TV, print ad, radio) and then takes action. The action isn't immediate (that is, "direct response"). Typically, this action involves going to a retailer to make the sale (or "convert"). The marketer has to hope that once the consumer sees/hears the message, they remember it. (Advertising studies show that the average consumer needs to see a message 7–8 times before it becomes familiar to them.) Branding is hard to measure. Typically, when determining branding success, the marketer will look at the anecdotal performance. A mar-keter looks at the timing the marketing campaign and any correlation in sales spikes that might have occurred during that specific time period. Performance for the most part is assumption driven.

Call to Action—A common direct response marketing term that simply means you're telling the reader what to do next, such as "click here now" or "call our 800 number today." Successful calls to action are usually related to scarcity, exclusivity, or timing (deadline).

Click-Through Rate (CTR)—This is the rate of clicks you get from the initial ad over to the landing page. The formula is number of clicks divided by the total impressions served (or audience size).

Control—This is a creative (or promotion) that is a proven winner and performs consistently.

Conversion Rate—The percentage of visitors who take a desired action.

Co Registration (CoReg)—A form of media buying in which you pur-chase a spot online in a location after a primary transaction occurs on the publisher's site. For instance, if someone signs up to receive informa-tion from the publisher (e-newsletters and so forth), after that sign-up is complete, your ad is then shown to the user along with ads from other advertisers who also have purchased a CoReg ad from the publisher. The key for CoReg to work is prompt, aggressive follow-through—leads from this source tend to go cold quickly because people often forget when and where they signed up from.

Cost Per Click (CPC)—This is another advertising model in which the advertiser is charged for each click. This is the basis for services like Google's AdWords.

Cost Per Lead (CPL)—This is another online advertising model in which the rate or cost is determined by the number of leads collected, as opposed to just clicks, as with CPC.

Cost Per Thousand (CPM)—A common online advertising model in which the rate is determined by the total number of impressions versus the CPM (1,000). A great, free CPM calculator to check out is www.clickz.com/cpm-calculator.

Creative—The term "creatives" refers to the creative element of an advertising or marketing campaign, such as the graphics and copywriting. This could pertain to both online and offline marketing tactics.

Direct Response Marketing—A form of marketing in which results are specific, quantifiable, and measurable. The DRM message generally is one strong message with a compelling offer delivered via a single platform (that is, an email, a newsletter ad, a direct letter, or an online ad). It's more controlled because you're directing the consumer where to go next (that is, "Click here now") and your message will be the only one in front of them at that time. You can directly calculate your ROI (return on investment), which helps the marketer offset any advertising costs from the profits. Plus, direct response marketing overall is typically more cost effective than branding. Some direct response metrics include open rate, click-through rate, response rate, conversion rate, break-even point (BEP), and return on investment (ROI).

Email List Rental—Renting the opportunity to send a dedicated email to a targeted email list. The publisher emails for you (you don't receive a file with email addresses). You send them your email and subject line. Rates here are usually higher, as your message is exclusive to the publisher's subscribers and email typically gets a lift note.

E-Newsletter Ads (or Sponsorships)—A paid ad spot with limited word count that appears in another publisher's e-newsletter. The ad links to a landing page. Ad rates are cheaper here than a dedicated email to the same list, since it's not exclusive content.

Guerrilla Marketing—A form of marketing whereby the marketer goes into social-based marketing platforms, such as message boards, forums, online bulletin boards, or blogs, and engages with users as well as plants strategic marketing messages.

Impressions—Impressions are the number of times a banner ad is exposed to potential eyes. The number of impressions is an important tool needed for a common rate model used in online advertising called CPM.

Insertion Order (IO)—This is the formal contract placed with an online advertiser or online ad network that has general information about the campaign such as timeframe, ad unit, ad model (CPC, CPM, CPL), and total number of impressions.

Interactive Advertising Bureau (IAB)—The Interactive Advertising Bureau is comprised of more than 460 leading media and technology companies who are responsible for selling 86% of online advertising in the United States. On behalf of its members, the IAB is dedicated to the growth of the interactive advertising marketplace, of interactive's share of total marketing spend, and of its members' share of total marketing spend. The IAB educates marketers, agencies, media companies, and the wider business community about the value of interactive advertising. For more information, visit www.iab.net

Landing Page—This is a web page that a user is redirected to. It's usually promotionally related and the goal can be for leads or sales.

Lead Generation (Lead Gen)—A form of Internet marketing in which the goal is to collect email address or names. Also called list building or prospecting efforts.

Lead Gen Page—Also known as a squeeze page. This is a webpage whose specific goal is email collection. Strong copy and call to action is critical for overall success.

Leaderboard—A banner ad unit with dimensions of 728x90 IMU. See Banner Ad Units.

Lift Note—A lift note is an introductory message at the top of an email or e-newsletter that helps boost or "lift" the overall response rate. This is primarily used when introducing something new to the list, such as a guest contributor, new advertiser, or other special message. It sets the tone and helps warm up the list.

Link Exchanges—When publishers agree to cross-link to each other's websites to help boost search engine rankings. This works best when the websites linking to each other are relevant (similar content), of good quality, and have good traffic rankings.

List—Also known as database, subscribers, names, and file. It is basically a publishers or companies prospects (leads) and customers (buyers).

LREC—See Rectangle.

Media Buying—Also known as advertising. It's the purchase of media from websites, radio, print magazines, or television (network, cable, and satellite). Media types and rates available vary on the channel and specific source.

Metadata—Metadata includes tags that are typically read by search engines, but some are also visible to the human reader. The data is usually in the HTML code of the web page. Metadata are descriptions and keywords that include Alt tags (images, graphics), title tags, meta description, and meta keywords. It may also include special codes to emphasize keywords that only search engines can read, such as H1 or H2 header codes.

Micro Site—A website or blog with a small amount of traffic and bad traffic ranking.

Online Ad Network—An agency that sells online advertising in bulk, across multiple niches, channels, and websites. Because you're buying media from a network as opposed to directly with the website, typically the bulk discount of the network gets passed down to the advertiser. Popular online ad networks include: Yahoo!, Advertising.com, Adbrite.com, 24/7 Real Media, Value Click, Tribal Fusion, and BlogAds.

Online Advertising—See Media Buying.

Open Ad Server (OAS)—This is an online ad server that the advertiser can usually access via real time to see how their online banner ad campaign is performing by looking at key stats, including click-through rates and impressions served.

Open Rate—This is the rate that an email is opened. The determining factor here is the subject line. A reader will see a subject line that determines if they will open the email to read the full content. The formula here is the amount of emails opened divided by the amount of emails sent.

Out Clause—Also known as termination right, it's common in online advertising insertion orders and contracts that specify the advertiser can stop the campaign at a given time (if it's not performing well) and only be charged for the ad units served.

Pay-Per-Click (PPC)—Also known as Cost Per Click (CPC), PPC is a form of online advertising. Most well known is Google's AdWords, in which advertisers buy a small text display ad, select keywords, create a budget, and manage the campaign. The advertiser is then charged "per click" for each ad. Rates range on popularity of the keywords associated with each ad created.

Rectangle—A type of banner ad. Rectangle ads can be medium (300x250 IMU) or large—also known as LREC (336x280 IMU)—although large rectangles have recently become delisted by the Interactive Advertising Buerau (IAB), as they are no longer common.

Remnant Space—This is leftover space that a website has and will typically try to unload at a deeply discounted rate. It's important to ask about remnant space when conducting media buys with either websites or online ad networks.

Roll Out—This is when a creative (or promotion) showed promising "test" results and now you're launching it to a larger distribution.

Run-Of-Network (RON)—Paying for one price and getting impressions that are served anywhere on the network (which could be several websites) the agency offers. Sites in the network are typically bundled by synergy.

Run-Of-Site (ROS)—Paying for one price and getting impressions that are served anywhere on the website within the main pages. Not highly targeted, so the rates are usually the cheapest for this term of ad effort.

SEM—Search engine marketing is using search engines (organic search results) to help gain website exposure and traffic.

SEO—Search engine optimization. Pertains to using targeted keywords in your website's "tags" (or descriptions that search engines read when they index your page). In addition to tags, other SEO tactics include keyword density, sorting like-minded content into groups to form lists, and enhancing (bold, underline, or italicizing) keywords and phrases.

SMM—Social media marketing. Pertains to the practice of marketing in social network communities with like-minded individuals. The underlying premise is to engage (interact) community members on a "friendly" social level to promote bonding. From a business standpoint, the goal is typically to help gain exposure, visibility, website traffic, leads, and brand-loyalty.

Solo Email—Also known as a dedicated email. This is a single, focused email message as opposed to an e-newsletter, in which a publisher is sharing their message (or real estate) with other messages.

Test—This is a creative (or promotion) that has not been proven.

Text Ad—Also known as contextual ad or display ad. An ad consisting of limited text, similar to Pay-Per-Click (PPC), but appear on websites or blogs and links to a landing page. A text ad can also appear in an e-newsletter. The advertising model can be on a cost per thousand (CPM) or cost per acquisition (CPA) basis.

Web 2.0—A term coined in recent years pertaining to interactive, social-based marketing where both publisher and user engage with each other. The platform is dynamic instead of static, meaning it is always changing.

White Hat SEO—These are industry best practices or "good." This includes search engine marketing techniques that are ethical and recommended, such as relevant/quality back-links, quality/relevant content, proper keyword use and tagging (including metadata), and keyword research.

Wide Skyscraper—A type of banner ad unit with dimensions 160x600 IMU. See Banner Ad Units.

Index

FREE Online Edition

Your purchase of **Content is Cash** includes access to a free online edition for 45 days through the Safari Books Online subscription service. Nearly every Que book is available online through Safari Books Online, along with more than 5,000 other technical books and videos from publishers such as Addison-Wesley Professional, Cisco Press, Exam Cram, IBM Press, O'Reilly, Prentice Hall, and Sams.

SAFARI BOOKS ONLINE allows you to search for a specific answer, cut and paste code, download chapters, and stay current with emerging technologies.

Activate your FREE Online Edition at www.informit.com/safarifree

> **STEP 1:** Enter the coupon code: NFSYZAA.

> **STEP 2:** New Safari users, complete the brief registration form. Safari subscribers, just log in.

If you have difficulty registering on Safari or accessing the online edition, please e-mail customer-service@safaribooksonline.com